as I am

as I am

ABBA BEFORE & BEYOND

AGNETHA FÄLTSKOG
WITH BRITA ÅHMAN

Acknowledgements

The publishers would like to thank Olle Rönnbäck at Polar Music and John Spalding
at Bocu for all their help.

First published in Great Britain in 1997 by

Virgin Publishing

332 Ladbroke Grove

London W10 5AT

First published in 1996 in Sweden by Norstedts

Copyright © 1996 Brita Åhman

Translated from Swedish by Alpha International Translations.

Inside photographs supplied by Brita Åhman (pp. 11, 13, 92, 93, 94,102,105, 109, 110 118, 146); Agnetha
Fältskog Private Collection (pp.18, 20, 22, 23, 24, 25, 26, 29, 34); Tobjörn Calvero
(pp. 34, 44, 48, 98, 126); Denise Grünstein (pp. 6, 138); Charles
Hammarsten (p.80); Robin Moderatho (pp. 8, 141, 142, 144); Pressens Bild
(pp.53, 56, 64, 68, 96, 130) ; Reportagebild (pp.28, 36, 42, 45, 68, 78, 85);
Studio Hansa; Svenskt Pressfoto (p.136); Retna (pp.32, 39); Pictorial Press
(pp.47, 50, 51, 52, 53, 58, 59, 60, 62, 65, 66, 70, 72, 73, 75, 76, 79, 80, 82, 85, 86,
87, 88, 95, 101, 112, 115); London Features; Polar Music (pp.14, 16, 61, 67, 69, 71,
83, 88, 90) IBL Bildbyrå (pp.31, 44); Kamerareportage (p.38).

Every effort has been made to trace and clear copyright of the images reproduced in
this book. If any ommisions have occured an acknowledgement will be made in
future editions.

A catalogue record for this book is available from the British Library.

ISBN 1 85227 654 1

Designed by Blackjacks, London
Printed by Lego, Italy.

To the ones I love – Linda and Christian

PREFACE

When it became clear that Brita Åhman was going to write this book about me and Norstedts wanted to publish it, I gave a great deal of thought as to where I would set the boundaries. How deeply should I go? How honest should I be? What should I shed light on and what should I keep to myself? What balance should I strike?

For example, I don't want to reveal anything about the men in my life. There will be no details about why my relationships or marriage broke up. Now and again I mention Björn Ulvaeus because he is the father of my children. But I don't want to say anything about him or anyone else that might cause any hurt.

You see, I know all too well what I say can be misinterpreted.

Naturally, it's too soon to give a complete account of my life. Inferences can't yet be drawn, my path has not been determined. I shall have more experiences and pass many more milestones.

Some already exist, and I am happy to talk about them while my memory is still fresh and before I am engulfed by new developments or one of life's sudden vagaries. The title of the book, *As I Am*, is taken from one of my early LPs.

It can be interpreted in two ways; you may think it means I'm going to reveal all, but, if anything, it's a description of the kind of person I am - a little reserved. Actually, I had never imagined collaborating on a book about my life!

However, I'm tired of the image that's been applied to me over the years. So now I feel that I'd like to show a few glimpses of my life to my readers, something of my reality and some of my thoughts.

Ekerö, June. Agnetha Fältskog

INTRODUCTION

During the late summer of 1982 Agnetha Fältskog turned to me for advice regarding an open letter she had written to the press. She felt persecuted by incessant mendacious articles.

The letter was rewritten as an open debate article, receiving a great deal of attention. Both the Royal Family and Björn Borg, along with many other well-known people, joined in the debate. Even then I saw what a marked difference there was between the young woman I'd come to know and the picture the weeklies painted of her.

The following year we decided to write a book, but after a coach accident on the way home from London, in 1983, there followed a series of scandalous articles about Agnetha that led to her withdrawing into herself altogether. It wasn't possible to work, so I broke contracts with both a publisher and Agnetha.

Over time, the depictions of Agnetha Fältskog have become ever more distorted. So, in April 1995, when I proposed that we work on a new book together she gave me a resolute yes. We had never lost touch down the years and I've managed to make use of this in my writing.

Thank you for your trust in me, Agnetha.

Brita Åhman

NEW YEAR, EKERÖ

The sun was just setting, drenching the deep green firtops in an intense orange rose shimmer. As the sun rays hit a field of yellow wintry grass it lit up in the sharp light throwing cascades of glitter over the frosty ground. The fjord lay dreamily calm, shifting along the scale of ionic blue and icy grey, as clouds rose on the horizon. When the wind started to pick up, the surface of the water briefly became a thin sheen of grainy gold as the sun for a short moment peeped through an opening in the cloud cover.

'It looks like snow,' says Agnetha, and looks up at some heavy clouds which hang stubbornly above the fir trees. 'Even the air smells of snow.'

We celebrated New Year's Eve in peace and quiet at Agnetha's house. Linda had been invited to stay with friends and Christian was a bit out of sorts and had stayed at home. Before midnight we walked down to the stables, by the paddock, and watched the horses, who had fresh fodder in their hayracks. When Agnetha came to a stop close by, each and every one of them whinnied its recognition, rubbed their soft muzzles against her and nudged her for more treats. Her big black Newfoundland bitch padded along contentedly at our heels as we turned homeward again. From the stables the horses could be heard stamping the ground.

The high firs stood calm and silent, clothed in sparkling frost. Not the slightest breath of wind moved in the branches. A Nordic winter's night.

At midnight, we were going to listen to Jarl Kulle read Tennyson's 'Ring out wild, bells, to the wild sky', in his majestic voice. Immediately before it strikes twelve Agnetha frantically begins searching for a bottle of champagne. She finds a bottle of Roederer pink champagne. It's flat.

She rummages around in the larder to see if there is anything else hiding on the shelves, but gives up and, instead, comes back with a carafe of cold, pure spring water which she had drawn the day before, from a natural spring deep within the forest.

She laughs as we toast the New Year with pure spring water, exchange hugs and wish each other a happy new year. 'Surely, no one would believe this of me! Water on New Year's Eve!'

She dresses up warmly when we go out for a stroll on New Year's Day. She looks bushy tailed and bright eyed, her hair newly washed and curly. A headband is pulled deep over her brow and she has wrapped a large, soft, brown scarf around her neck. She dresses tastefully, fairly discreetly, often with a few original and fun touches. A strong contrast to the provocative stage costumes her audience have seen her in during her time with ABBA. A touch of make-up. Sparing with her jewellery, even for parties. She always wears a small, narrow gold ring on her right ring-finger – her mother's confirmation ring.

A fresh breeze blows from the bay. It bites into the cheeks and the birches bend down low in the wind. 'I take an awful lot of walks, often alone. I need this solitude since Mother and Father's untimely passing. I derive enormous pleasure from the air and the beauty of Nature and being so close to the memorial park in the cemetery. It gives me peace and fulfilment.'

We walk there at a leisurely pace and chat about everything between Heaven and Earth. Just like most people on New Year's Day, Agnetha wonders what the new year will bring. Order? Chaos?

'I think of the last few years and they haven't been kind to me,' says Agnetha. 'My mother's passing away and my second divorce. At the same time my father fell ill and in the new year of 1996 he passed away, too. Within the space of two years I lost both of my parents. The loneliness weighs heavily upon me.

'It's also a tough world for children to grow up and live in. Ever increasing violence and war that never ends. The absurdity of humanity's advances. We destroy our own environment: earth; sea; atmosphere. How could we destroy nature, leaving behind a ravaged planet for our children and grandchildren?'

When Agnetha gets upset her eyes become a deeper blue. She is not so gracious when she gets angry. Anyone who's been close to her knows that. Behind the soft blonde exterior there are the claws of a tiger. They can scratch hard.

There are also happier topics; her children. As a single mother, Agnetha can take pleasure in having succeeded so well with them. However, Linda and Christian have, themselves, healthy attitudes. And a lot of gumption!

'Linda has become an excellent horsewoman and has her own mounts in the stables at home on the farm. She's a very sweet, straightforward and lively young woman, who has matured a lot in the last few years. Competitive riding, however, was not her choice of profession, despite many successes in competitions around the country, to which I've often driven her, horse box and all.

'She wants to be an actress and is putting her heart and soul into it. She's done well at drama school and hasn't been afraid to work hard backstage, as a dresser amongst other

things. I hope she makes it. It's a tough career, but she's done very well so far. She has a strong will and personality. Stubborn, too. That's important.

'Currently she has a part in Björn and Benny's musical *Kristina Fran Duvemala*. It was a fantastic experience for her to be a part of the fabulous premièr in October 1995, the euphoria, the volleys of applause and the subsequent success.

'Christian is gifted in a number of ways. Part of him is definitely artistic. When he was little he used to do the most fantastic drawings and paintings, often with a story. He is also musically talented, after Björn and I; it had fully blossomed when he was young. He played the organ and synthesiser and composed songs, which he sang with a clear voice and perfect pitch. We won't be surprised if he gives music a go some time in the future. But he is also strikingly analytical and has chosen to study natural sciences at upper secondary school. The synth has been replaced by the computer. It's been very stimulating to follow his and Linda's development during the past few years.

'I try not to push them in any particular direction, but to support them in whatever they choose to do. I'm there for them at all times.

'One thing I have made a point of is not to spoil them too much, despite my resources. As a single mother it could have been easy, during my career, to compensate for long absences with loads of expensive presents and bits and pieces.

'I do use my money to give them a healthy, lavish, wonderful environment to live in. A pool, stables, a jetty on the water and wide open spaces in the countryside. Also the best possible education. I do not consider these unnecessary extravagances. The children have to learn to keep house; I want to be generous and provident in essential situations.'

When we get to the memorial garden we sit down a while. There's a fountain, encircled by pale granite, simply hewn in clean lines. Agnetha has placed a few candles there, which have been burning since New Year's Eve, and placed a beautiful wreath on the stone. A white hyacinth has managed to break through the frost and flower.

'I sense an air of calm here,' says Agnetha, 'there is space here and the fragrance of water and forest.'

We go into the 12th Century church where candles burn on the Christmas trees. They give off a clean aroma which mixes with the smell of old wood.

Agnetha stops next to an old organ which, unfortunately, is locked. She moves her slender fingers across it and suddenly says, 'I would like to play, perhaps train to be a cantor.'

Then she looks up toward the big church organ by the wall.

'I'd like to play a gigantic organ with five keyboards and pedals, with artistic adornments on the facade, like you see in really old churches. I can imagine myself giving recitals! Not for money, just for it's own sake, but there would probably be a few too many people,' she smiles.

By the baptismal font a few candles burn in the tall, sturdy iron candlesticks. We are alone here and sit down on the front pew. The silence is complete and comforting. The conversation turns, as a matter of course, to life and death. Mostly death. For long periods we sit in absolute silence.

Thoughts form. Again, Agnetha talks about the sense of loss she feels for her parents. 'It's so difficult to accept that the people who've meant so much to you, in your life, aren't around. My soul aches. Emptiness. I miss them so much, I'm trying to work on my sorrow but it's a wound I'll carry with me for the rest of my life.

'During some bright, hopeful moments I've felt that their souls have found one another, somewhere much greater than we can imagine. The eternal light. I truly hope it's so.'

Agnetha, with father Ingvar, mother Birgit and little sister Mona.

CONNIE FRANCIS WAS MY GREAT IDOL

SHE WAS EASY TO IMITATE IN FRONT OF THE BEDROOM MIRROR

She clambers carefully up on to the high piano stool. She's five years-old, blonde plaited hair, cornflower blue eyes. A small gap between her teeth. She settles herself.

Tentatively she begins to play, with just her right hand. Suddenly she finds a melody. She repeats it many times. Then she begins to sing, making up her own words; 'Two small trolls...'

Agnetha laughs at the memory and hums the melody. Yes, that was actually her first 'song', the first time she realised that she could make up her own little tunes. She remembers the feeling. Once she'd realised that she could do it, she kept on picking out melodies and making up lyrics.

Agnetha Ase Fältskog was born in Jonkoping on 5 April 1950. The year that the British Empire ended in India, after 178 years, and the independent Republic of India was founded. Coffee-rationing finally came to an end in Sweden, after the war. The invention of the Century, television, was well under way. The Korean War was starting.

Jonkoping, in Smaland, was a small, idyllic but simultaneously vigorous town at the southern tip of Lake Vattern's shore, a dominion town and the seat of Gote's Court of Appeal.

A number of large industries were to be found there, including engineering workshops and Svenska Tandsticks AB (Swedish Matches Ltd) which created the institution, Solstickan (The Sun Matchstick) in 1936. This collected funds to support invalid care and medical services as well as research through a price supplement on matchboxes with a special label which was to become world famous: a little naked boy, running with blond hair flying out behind him, as drawn by one of Sweden's most famous artists, Einar Nerman.

The western quarter of Jonkoping's centre was founded in about 1850, featuring characteristic two storey wooden buildings. The eastern part was founded as far back as the beginning of the 17th Century and contains the town's oldest buildings, including the Court of Appeal. The Fältskog family lived near Ostra Storgatan on Tegelbruksgatan, immediately next to Lake Vattern.

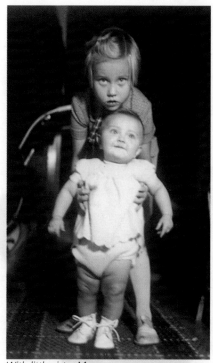

With little sister Mona.

Agnetha lived in this town until she was eighteen, with its robust mixture of industry and culture, in a small but cosy home. She went to school, Sunday school, sang and performed in church, played and got into mischief with her friends – and started along the road as a singer.

As she grew up she became more serious about composing music. Agnetha has books full of tunes and lyrics from those years, all packed away in the cellar.

When she first started playing she didn't have her own piano, but the upstairs neighbour did. Agnetha would knock on the door and ask nicely if she might use it for a while. It became a daily request.

The dream, of course, was to have her own piano. She felt she waited forever, but on her seventh birthday there it was, her present from her mother and father: a beautiful, polished, brown piano with black and white keys that begged to be played.

Now she could begin piano lessons. It was only when she started these that she enjoyed her first simple but concrete experience of music. She'd begun to learn notes, right hand for these, left hand for those, but she had trouble with co-ordination. Each hand was fine on its own, but it was tricky to get them working together! Until one day it suddenly clicked: the sounds had synchronised. It became a complete melody with treble and bass. It was a real kick!

By the time Agnetha was fourteen, her piano teacher felt that she could teach her nothing more. By then she could play both the piano and the harpsichord. She often played Bach's fugues on the church harpsichord, but she absorbed all kinds of music: classical, jazz, pop and folk.

From early childhood she was surrounded by musical sounds. Her mother had a good voice and her father, Ingvar, was especially musically gifted. He was the neighbourhood variety king, he had started his own ballet troupe and was an enthusiastic supporter of amateur dramatics. He wrote lyrics and sketches which were performed in the town and its

School has started.

Agnetha graduates from lower secondary school.

environs. His creativity was endless, whilst he was also dedicated to his job. Around Christmas time, he would usually set up seasonal plays. He played the guitar and sang at various events, which Agnetha often attended.

Her parents were very different from each other. Her mother was gentle and introverted while her father was dynamic and outgoing. Her mother was a true housewife, the

family anchor: always available. Yet both Agnetha's parents backed her musical interests. So childhood, with them and sister Mona, was happy, safe and uncomplicated.

I took the four year course at junior secondary school. I was good at languages and music, but I didn't do so well in maths, physics or chemistry. So after I took the lower school exam I left with bad grades in those subjects and good ones in Swedish, English, German and music.

There was a celebration on the day we got our results and grey graduation cap. I thought it was brilliant that I'd done it, but I was sure I didn't want to carry on to upper secondary school. I was fifteen and tired of school. I wanted to be free for a while and then get a job somewhere.

So I looked around and got a job at Atteviks car dealership as an office girl and switchboard operator. It was fun and I liked it just fine. Every morning I walked to work. It was a really long way, and when it rained I would sometimes arrive wet through. I ran errands and sat on the switchboard all day. I couldn't care less what work I did as long as I made some money and could carry on with my music.

I had two girlfriends that I sang with. We formed a band and called ourselves The Cambers. We sang at New Year revues and sometimes at parties. I wrote some songs which we sang in parts. We were quite pushy and occasionally sent tapes to Sveriges Radio. The reply arrived pretty quickly. 'No thank you.' With the postscript, 'Don't call us we'll call you!'

Connie Francis was my great idol. She was easy to imitate, in songs such as 'Who's Sorry Now?' and 'My Happiness', in front of the little dressing mirror in my room. I'd listen for hours on end, etching the words,

The Cambers.

music and timbre into my mind. I taught myself the phrasing, and to breathe in exactly the same manner as Connie.

Later, I did the same thing with other favourites like Petula Clark, Cilla Black, Sandie Shaw, Rita Pavone and Dusty Springfield. I played records by Neil Sedaka & P.J. Proby, The Beatles, The Beach Boys and Herb Alpert and The Tijuana Brass over and over again. I could never get enough.

When I heard one day that Bernt Enghardt's dance band, in Huskvarna, was looking for a singer I called up immediately and asked for an audition. Bernt had announced a new singer called Agnetha but just as she was about to start performing she fell ill. So I got to audition.

I could tell that they liked me but they said that they had three or four more people to look at. So I had to wait for an answer. And then it came; they had chosen me.

My portrait was quickly pasted over the other Agnetha's picture on the already printed posters, and I started at once. I was fifteen years old.

Of course my mother wondered how it would work out combining a full-time job with singing, and wanted to know how many gigs we were talking about. I settled her mind by saying it was only on weekends!

'But, shouldn't you have a life too?,' she wondered, 'Going out and enjoying yourself?'

'No, I'm going to sing.'

When I told the band that I wrote my own songs their ears pricked up. They liked them too. So one of the guys arranged them and we rehearsed them. I had all sorts of different material. Mostly I wrote when I was a little down, when it was over with some guy. That's when the songs came to me.

I composed 'Jag var sa kar' (*I Was So In Love*) and 'Utan dig' (*Without You*), and they proved so popular that we used to play them as the last dance.

Agnetha and Bernt Enghardt's orchestra pose for a picture.

Smålands Folkblad

Måndagen den 22 januari 1968

Jönköpingsflicka

MOT SVENSK- TOPPEN

Local newspaper realises what is happening. The headline reads:
'Jonkoping girl heads for the Swedish hit parade.'

UNGDOMS-

SUDDENLY, ONE DAY THE PHONE RANG

IT WAS LITTLE GERHARD FROM THE RECORD COMPANY CUPOL, IN STOCKHOLM

We didn't only perform in Jonkoping but travelled all over Smaland. We'd finish at one or two in the morning, sometimes later. Then we'd pack up, carry out the instruments and cram ourselves, six guys and myself, into a little car and drive home through the night.

Often I wouldn't creep into bed until four or five in the morning, only to get up, with the songs still in my head, at seven to start work at eight. It was obvious that working at the car dealer's was going to clash with the music. Over all it was neither particularly fun nor particularly demanding.

However, what could be more wonderful for a teenager than to stand in front of a microphone and sing languorous songs to an enthusiastic audience ?

One day I was so tired at work that I fainted and was sent home. My mother realised straight away that I was worn out, and told me, 'Now you've got to choose! You can't carry on like this.'

I, too, was well aware of that, so I gave in my notice.

The band was already a success. We were in such demand that we began working every night. Mother and Father never tried to stop me, which they could have done because I wasn't of age. They let me be. Frankly they knew it wasn't possible to stop me!

The important thing to me was to stand on stage and use my voice. Thankfully, my voice could easily cover a wide range. I sang everything, including jazz: 'I Feel Good', 'Hallelujah', 'I Just Love Him So....' Of course I dreamt of being a great singer, but at that time my aim wasn't to become a world famous star. I didn't think for a moment that I ever would be, but I hoped to make a record. Maybe get into the Swedish charts.

Then, yet another piece of luck helped me along that road, for at the record company Cupol, later bought out by CBS Stockholm, there was an alert and progressive talent scout who called himself Little Gerhard. That was his stage name during a short but intense period as a rock 'n' roll star in Sweden in the 50s. His real name was Karl-Gerhard Lundkvist and he was always on the lookout for new talent. Bernt, who had met Little Gerhard, wrote to him saying that he played with a good gang of musicians, had a capable young singer and asked if he could send a tape. That was fine with the scout.

We went to a little studio in Eksjo and recorded a few numbers, including some of mine, among them 'Jag var sa kar'. We also sent a picture of us all, along with our names.

Her whole life in front of her.

Out of the blue the phone rang at home. It was Little Gerhard from Stockholm. So he said! I couldn't believe it was true. No way! Little Gerhard wouldn't call me! When it became clear that he was only interested in me, not the band, I became really suspicious.

It's just someone who wants to tease me, I thought. Perhaps one of the guys from the band testing my loyalty.

Little Gerhard laughed his head off and said, 'OK, if you don't believe me, here's my number. You call me then!' So, I rang.

He invited me to Stockholm to record two of my own songs as singles. It was really very painful that they only wanted me and not Bernt Enghardt's band. For three years I'd sung with his band and now they weren't included, even though it was Bernt who'd come up with the idea of sending the tape to Cupol. I felt terrible, but everyone understood that I couldn't turn down such a wonderful opportunity.

I didn't stop singing with Bernt's band straight away, as has been written, but carried on for as long as I could; right up until I left Jonkoping. It was obvious I was off to Stockholm.

My father was enthusiastic right from the word go, and said that he would travel with me. We would stay at my aunt's. I could hardly sleep the night before we left. I got up early, showered, and washed my hair.

'I'll be the cleanest person in the world ,' I thought.

I sat with Father on the train out of Jonkoping full of expectation and dreadfully nervous. It was an ordinary, gloomy October's day, but I wouldn't have cared if there had been a monsoon.

When we walked into Philips House, where the recordings were to be made, I felt like an awkward country lass who'd come to the big city. I was so new to all of this. The nervousness I felt was different to the way I would later feel with ABBA. Then, it would be because the expectations were so high.

On the stairs down to the studio, I suddenly heard the backing to my songs being recorded by Sven-Olof

Little Gerhard – Agnetha's discoverer and friend.

Walldorf's Orchestra. My songs! They were laying down the strings. My heart missed a beat. What a blast! It was an enormous moment in my life. The director was absolutely delighted and everyone was really kind and helpful. They had great hopes and said that it wasn't often that Cupol gambled on two singles by a new and inexperienced singer. That didn't exactly help me to relax.

They thought that I sounded like a new Connie Francis, which wasn't too odd considering how much I'd listened to her and mimed in front of the mirror at home. They were surprised when they heard that I could change the pitch of my voice. But then again I would have sung backwards if they had wanted! Straight after the recording, Father and I travelled home to Jonkoping and I continued to sing with the band a while longer.

One morning, as the family sat round the breakfast table, I suddenly heard my own voice on the radio. I took the radio in my arms and danced around with it. I'll never forget it! When I look back now that was one of the happiest moments in my whole working life, even compared to all the subsequent successes with ABBA.

Things hotted up. The two singles, 'Jag var sa kar' and 'Utan dig' became my first hits, and were soon followed by my first LP, which had a lot of my own material on it. Not only did I appear in the Swedish charts, but I was soon ahead of The Beatles in Swedish sales.

It was suggested that I should move to Stockholm. I was quick to say yes although it was a big step for me. After all, my roots were in Jonkoping. My family, friends, Bernt and the band were all there. I was no more than eighteen when I made the move and headed for our capital city. It was pretty courageous and I sometimes wonder why I wasn't more uneasy about it. How could I have known it would be all right? Was I just naive?

But I've never felt any fear when it comes to work; one step comes naturally after the other. I've been lucky; things have always fallen into place in that area of my life.

Agnetha's first real 'collector's card'.

HE HAD A CHARMING VOICE

AND WAS AN ARTIST, LIKE ME. I SENSED THAT WE WERE MARITALLY COMPATIBLE

Once Agnetha had reached the top of the Swedish charts with 'Jag var sa kar' everything moved very quickly. After further success in Sweden the record company decided to launch her in West Germany, through a record company called Hansa Schallplatten.

She had got good grades in languages at junior secondary school, including German, so there was no problem singing in that tongue. The producer was a young man who'd had some success with his own songs. He looked after her and was her safe haven in Berlin.

Love seemed inevitable: blonde, pretty nineteen-year-old, already a star in her own country, moves abroad for the first time and has her career helped along by a cute producer in the German record business. Engagement was just around the corner.

Agnetha released eight singles in German, but never had a breakthrough there. They weren't interested in releasing her compositions, either, which disappointed her, of course. She thinks that 'Utan dig' would have gone down well, but they didn't take to the suggestion. So it wasn't a successful excursion. The engagement was broken off after barely a year.

On her arrival back in Sweden, Agnetha received a letter from the television producer Kage Gimtell of Sveriges Radio in Malmo. He asked if she would like to take part in a Jules Sylwain gala on television, which he was calling *Rakna de Lyckliga stunderna blott* (*Only Count The Happy Moments*).

When she saw some of the participants listed, it gave her a shock: Sten Nilsson, Agneta Munther, Agnetha Fältskog and – Björn Ulvaeus.

She had already met Björn during some 'people's park' tours. Once he was supposed to appear after her with the Hootenanny Singers. However, she arrived late and the Hootenanny Singers had to step into her spot. It really irritated Björn, so things at this stage were distinctly chilly between them.

Björn had released his first solo single, which was called 'Raring' (Darling). I thought he was cute, became interested, and asked for a copy of his single. It came by return post. We fell deeply in love during a television recording on the west coast in May 1969.

Björn was warm and tender. I looked up to him. He was well read and intelligent, very well informed and at home with most things.

I wasn't. I had done nothing, since leaving school, to improve myself. I see that as a shortcoming.

He had a charming voice and was an artist, like me. I felt that we were maritally compatible, which is quite apparent in some of the pictures from that time!

Benny and Frida met in 1970 on a radio show recording. As Benny and Björn were working as a duo, it wasn't long before their girlfriends met. The foursome soon began working together.

An early tour.

Benny and Frida became engaged in August 1969, and a few months later we followed suit. We all went off to Cyprus and had a terrific engagement party.

Björn and I had found a flat on Lilla Essingen. We moved in and began to look for the right church for our wedding.

In April 1971 Björn, Benny and I formed a trio and set off on a tour of 'people's parks', while Frida toured with Lasse Berghagen.

There were many breaks for recording during that period. I made my fourth album, 'Nar en vacker tanke blir en sang' (*When A Beautiful Thought Becomes A Song*), with Björn as producer. Before that Little Gerhard had worked on my first two albums, 'Agnetha Fältskog' and 'Agnetha Fältskog Vol. 2', at Metronome's Studio.

On the third album 'Som jag ar' (*As I Am*), which included my own song 'Om tarar vore guld' (*If Tears*

Were Made Of Gold), I'd asked Björn to be co-producer along with Gerhard. That album included a duet with Björn called, significantly enough, 'Sa har borjar karlek' (*This Is How Love Begins*).

At this point all four of us thought it was time to give our first floorshow together a try. We called it 'Festfolket' (*The Party People*), and began rehearsals. It was not a success, generally comprising of a thin spread of vapid jokes and other people's songs.

The premier, at Tradgar'n restaurant in Gothenburg, saw a few scattered couples at tables in an otherwise empty auditorium. It could have meant a premature end for the budding ABBA quartet.

Then we decided to take our show to Strand in Stockholm, and started using Björn and Benny's 'Hej gamle man' (*Hello Old Man*), from their album 'Lycka' (*Happiness*), which also included 'Liselott', a song Björn and I had written the lyrics to. 'Hej gamle man' became a showpiece in the Strand show. A song from Frida's album, 'Tre kvart fran nu' (*Three Quarters Of An Hour From Now*) lifted things, too. Frida and I really pushed 'Hej gamle man' and it became a hit as soon as it came out. It was the first record with all four of us on it. The pieces of ABBA had begun to fall into place.

After the show at Strand it would be a while before we all worked together again, apart from doing backing vocals for each other. All of us were focusing on our individual careers. My solo career was at its peak. I had also got my first theatrical role as Mary Magdalene in the Swedish production of Tim Rice and Andrew Lloyd Webber's rock opera *Jesus Christ Superstar*. It had been a long-time dream of mine to act. Now I had my chance,

and didn't intend to let it pass me by. I delighted in being on stage and it was a success from the start. I recorded the main song, 'Vart ska min karlek fora' (*I Don't Know How To Love Him*), a quiet and sensitive song, and it became very popular.

Frida was also on her way up at the time. She was marvellous on her first album, with Benny on piano and producing. Both Benny and Björn were actively supporting us in our careers.

Benny had left The Hepstars and Björn's participation in the Hootenanny Singers was on the wane. Instead they had begun a creative collaboration which would result in some of the pop world's most brilliant songs and lyrics, eventually true classics – and multi-million sellers.

They formed their own company, Union Songs, with Stig 'Stikkan' Anderson. During the 60s and 70s Stikkan had made his name as a popular tunesmith and lyricist. Michael B. Tretow, engineer and gifted sound technician, joined the team, becoming responsible for recording. Stikkan Anderson and Bengt Bernhag had started another company in 1963 called Polar Music. When Bengt tragically passed away in 1971, Björn and Benny began to work as Stikkan's partners in the company.

Björn and I continued to write lyrics together, 'Kungens vaktparad' (Parade Of The King's Guard) and 'Mitt sommarland' (My Summer Holiday Country), were played all over the country that year.

During a tour of 'people's parks' we found the perfect place for our wedding, a romantic old church in the village of Verum in northern Skane. We knew immediately that this was the place we'd dreamed of and searched for.

The small 17th Century gothic church was packed, with the cream of the Swedish pop world as specially invited celebrities. The smell of flowers pervaded the air and the warmth of the candles spread as everyone waited for the bride and groom to arrive. Parents and relatives all dressed up and fidgeting sat on the front rows of the pews.

Agnetha as Mary Magdalene in Jesus Christ Superstar, staged at Scandinavium in Gothenburg.

Over three thousand people had gathered outside to see the wedding of the year, between Agnetha Fältskog and Björn Ulvaeus, on 6 July 1971.

For many years Agnetha had completely captivated Sweden's population. Björn had many of fans from his time with The Hootenanny Singers. He had also sung himself into Swedish hearts with his versions of the wonderful songs by Dan Anderson from the forests of Dalarna, amongst others 'Jag vantar vid min mila' (*I'm Waiting By My Charcoal Pile*) and 'Dar bjorkarna susa' (*Where The Birches Sough*), and had enjoyed great success with his album 'Raring'.

The fans outside the church jostled to catch a glimpse of their idols, press photographers fought to get the best angles. When Agnetha arrived, in an open landau drawn by a team of white horses, there was a great commotion. Her wedding dress was a 'dream in white' and in her long blonde hair she had a garland of white flowers.

Her eyes shone and photographers took countless snaps of the smiling bride. These adorned the covers of most of the country's weeklies within days. Here were all the ingredients for a romantic fairy tale wedding, as though designed for magazine readers.

The guests inside the church didn't see that one of the horses was made nervous by the tumult, and happened to stamp on Agnetha's foot as she stepped down from the landau, on her way into the church. It throbbed and hurt but she put on a brave face.

As she and Björn walked through the church doors Benny struck up Felix Mendelssohn's 'Wedding March', followed by his own composition 'Wedding'. Little did he imagine then, that later in life he would be compared to the great masters.

The marriage service could begin.

Björn was formerly in the Hootenanny Singers. They released over 30 singles and 16 albums between 1964 and 1975. So popular were they that in 1966, young conscripts Björn and the other two band members were granted leave from the army to continue playing music, provided that they kept up their military training at the same time.

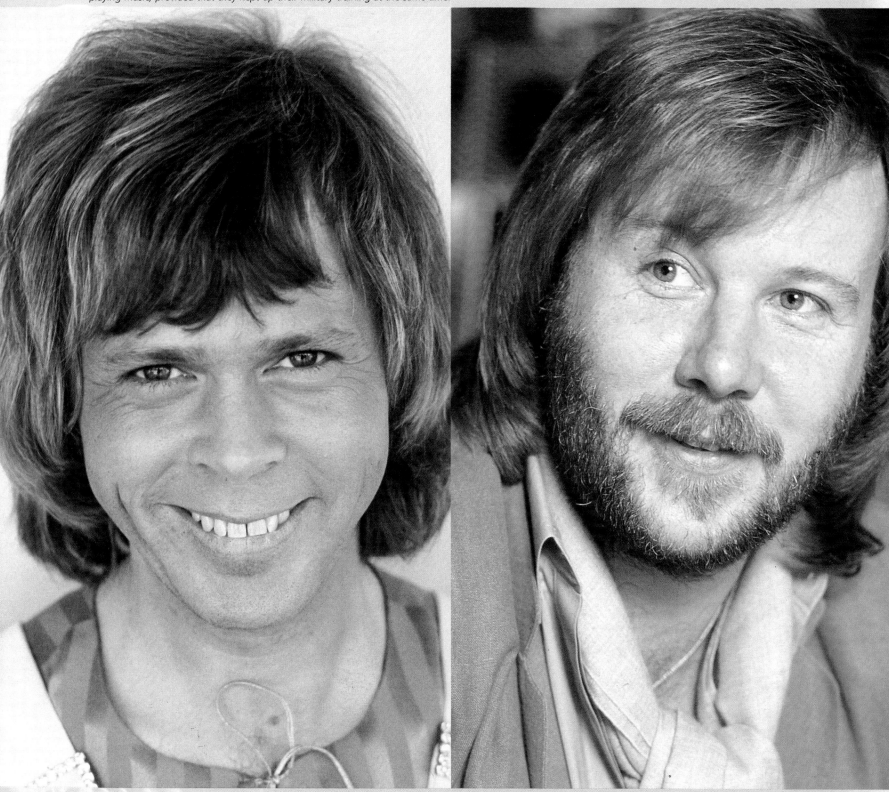

Benny was the keyboard player of the Hep Stars, one of Scandinavia's biggest bands. They released over 20 singles and 10 albums from 1964 to 1970. Two retrospective compilations followed later.

Agnetha expecting her first child, Linda, who was born 23rd February 1973.

IT WAS
GOOD THEN

It was good then. I felt secure and we had a few really good years. We wanted a family and planned children from the start, but no baby came along. Around the time we moved to Vallentuna I began to go for tests. Every month I was disappointed when nothing happened. We even thought about adoption and contacted the Adoption Agency. However, regulations stated that you had to be twenty-five to adopt, so we were too young - I was only twenty-one then.

I have always had strong maternal instincts. Even when I was still a child I cut out pictures of prams from newspapers and imagined the feeling of pushing my own pram through fresh winter snow and seeing the wheels' tracks behind me in the road.

When I eventually became pregnant, two years later, I could hardly believe it. I had been worried, so I'll never forget when I picked up the test and it was positive. I rang Björn and yelled down the phone, 'We're going to have a baby!'

He was overjoyed and came straight home with a bottle of champagne. I rushed out and threw my arms around him. We laughed and cried by turns; we were so happy!

Benny and Frida moved into the neighbourhood and we saw a lot of each other. The boys got on with writing and we stayed in, round at each other's houses, singing and playing. So, you could say that ABBA formed quite naturally. After all, we had the same jobs, and our mutual interests in music brought us together.

Articles have postulated that Frida and I hated each other from the start which is, in fact, pure nonsense. On the contrary, we saw a lot of each other out there in Vallentuna. Later, during our ABBA career, we always supported each other on stage. If one of us wasn't on form, the other stepped in and took over.

On the other hand, I admit there was a strong sense of competition within both of us. Therefore the songs were full of energy and tension. We fought over the audience and that gave an extra kick to the concerts.

The interesting aspect of the ABBA sound was created by our differences. As far as we could, we made the most of our respective voices.

In the book ABBA *The Complete Recording Sessions*, by Carl Magnus Palm, Benny says: 'When you talk about the ABBA sound you have to consider how we arranged the songs, Michael's input and so on. But take away Frida and Agnetha and let two other girls sing instead and the ABBA sound goes out the window. Their voices were, quite simply, the most important component in the whole of our sound structure.'

I don't want to hide the fact that Frida and I had opposite backgrounds, temperaments and personalities. Neither did we get psyched up or wind down in the same way. We could get furious and tired with each other, so we had our moments but, surely, it would have

been strange if we didn't. It went on between all the members of the group.

We worked at a killing pace while we crossed continents and timezones, never catching up sleep before we started work again. Fatigue sometimes caused severe irritation. The intensity meant that we had no control. When it was at its height I wanted us to ease off the pace a bit.

We had a great capacity for work, so if we'd slowed down a little bit we could have easily gone on for another ten years.

When we went on television to do 'Ring Ring', in the qualifying round of the Eurovision Song Contest, on the 10th February 1973, I was expecting, enormous. I was overdue by a few days so it was a little risky. I wasn't too stressed out myself but everyone around me was more or less hysterical, especially one of the studio hostesses.

On one occasion she happened to hear a child shriek, came storming down the corridor and yelled, 'Oh, my goodness, has it arrived?' She thought I'd had my baby in the middle of the television studio!

We gave a good performance and the audience reaction was tumultuous. Everyone tipped us to win. But the jury had a different opinion.

'Ring Ring' wasn't a great song, but it was successful in Sweden and across Scandinavia. In Britain, on the other hand, it was a flop. We were unknown there then.

To me, at least, it was a stroke of luck that we only came third with 'Ring Ring'. Linda was born on the 23rd February, so I could devote myself to her and avoid the whirlwind of activity that a success would have meant.

For that matter, perhaps it was lucky for all four of us. It gave us time to prepare for the future.

A FEW IMPORTANT YEARS

TO SUDDENLY SEE EVERYTHING THAT WE'D WORKED FOR ALL THOSE YEARS BECOME REALITY WAS BEWILDERING AND INDESCRIBABLE

When 'Ring Ring' came out it had Agnetha's, Benny's, Björn's and Anni-Frid's christian names on the cover. That was long and ungainly. So, when 'Waterloo' was released at the beginning of 1974, to get a build up in Europe before The Eurovision Song Contest, the name 'ABBA' emerged for the first time on a cover, but for safety's sake with the parenthesis: Björn, Benny, Agnetha & Frida.

Björn and Benny had begun working together as a team. Agnetha, who had her song 'Disillusion' included on their 'Ring Ring' LP, was in full swing composing the songs for her own album 'Elva kvinnor i ett hus' (*Eleven Women In A House*). Agnetha's Swedish version of 'S.O.S.' was on the album but the rest of the material was her own.

The demands on her as composer, author and singer had become so high that she delegated Bosse Carlgren as writer. She felt it best to concentrate on the music and singing, but did produce herself for the first time.

The collaboration with CBS-Cupol continued without any hitches. They had introduced her when she was only seventeen and respected and liked her. That made it easy for them to work together.

Of course, they still wanted to make new records with her, despite ABBA's success, but Stikkan was opposed. He found it hard to swallow that she wasn't tied to Polar and it irritated him that Polar were forced to buy her out. He later fell out with ABBA after the Swedish inland revenue investigated their tax affairs, and the band lost a couple of million each because of his poor management.

On 9 February the Swedish qualifying heats of the Eurovision Song Contest were broadcast on Swedish television and ABBA celebrated a runaway victory for 'Waterloo'. 'Ring Ring' had also been a tremendous hit and that reinforced the success. So it was an optimistic quartet of lovers who set sail for England's south coast and Brighton in 1974.

The weather was lousy when they arrived. The waves crashed on to the famed resort's stony beach and the rain pelted down. It was 6 April, and ABBA were to try their luck in the Eurovision Song Contest.

They booked into The Grand Hotel, which was near The Dome where the final would take place in front of five hundred million television viewers, and tried on their 'groovy' costumes and platform boots one last time.

Owe Sandstrom and Artistdressing who designed all of ABBA's costumes were careful to use beautiful material that would be comfortable to work in too. Agnetha wasn't sewn into her costume, as has been suggested, although it certainly was a tight fit.

Paste, embroidery, glitter and lustrous fabrics were the trend for pop stars, with artists such as David Bowie and Marc Bolan at the forefront of British glam rock. But in Sweden in the 70s gold lamé and pearls didn't pass muster anymore. Hobnailed boots and Palestinian shawls were the height of fashion to many people. It would be a while before the Swedes acknowledged the group at all. They showed no pride in ABBA's exceptional success. Instead they were strongly criticised and people poked fun at their costumes.

The passage of time means that what was once sniggered at has become a cult. Today no one need hide the fact that they like ABBA!

Back in 1974, the day of the competition flew by. Suddenly the wait was over and the moment had arrived. Sven-Olof Walldorf (Agnetha's friend from her very first records) stood there in full Napoleon get-up and raised his baton.

They were off. They had two minutes and forty six seconds. There was so much life in the song. The energy was so palpable you could touch it. They were sexy, fresh and – it would turn out – winners.

Remarkably, Agnetha's little blue sequinned cap, above her flying blonde hair, didn't blow off when she gave it her all. Sparks flew off her. Benny, the effervescent show man, who had played every instrument he could lay his hands on since he was a little lad, looked as though he was about to blast off from his piano stool.

It was as if a Viking ship had been launched, carrying the world's most famous Swedes. They ended up second only to Volvo as a Swedish export.

Many people believed that after their success in Brighton, ABBA would fade away like so many other shooting stars in the pop firmament. However, then Björn, Benny and Stikkan showed what they were capable of – 'S.O.S.' shot up the charts with a rapidity seldom seen in the history of pop music.

The starting gun for ABBA fever, throughout Europe, had been fired. It would continue for ten charged years and later, in the 90s, start up again.

It was just unbelievable when 'Waterloo' won! After the event a lot of people said that they felt it was unbeatable.

I had been none too sure about that. In order to get my head together and calm my nerves I started getting dressed and putting my make-up on early. I kept busy for a long while and was very thorough. I'd bought some small stars, which glittered beautifully, and glued them to my cheeks as a way of preparing myself; getting into 'character'.

Naturally I was very excited but I hadn't really convinced myself that we would do too well. My bet was that we would place in the top five, but certainly not win. After all we were complete unknowns in both Britain and Europe.

Olivia Newton-John, singing 'Long Live Love', was a hot favourite and the Dutch duo's entry, 'I See A Star', was also very good. I thought that they both had a better chance than 'Waterloo' which, frankly, I think was one of our poorer songs! However, it did have a powerful, stirring tempo and a melody that sticks in the mind. You could already hear people whistling it after the rehearsals.

As the results began to come in, it was very hard to sit still. We could hardly believe our eyes and ears as the points were read out and our victory became a fact.

Before we received the winning trophy there was a prize for the tune's composers: Björn, Benny and Stikkan. Stikkan was up on stage quickly, but Björn and Benny were stopped by some over-zealous security guards. So things were a bit confusing for a moment.

In the Eurovision Song Contest of 1974 'Waterloo' beat off the challenges of 'Si' by Gigliola Cinquetti (Italy), which came second, 'I See A Star' by Mouth & McNeal (Holland), which came third, and 'Long Live Love' by Olivia Newton-John (UK), which came joint fourth with Monaco and Luxembourg. The odds on ABBA to win were 20 to 1. Benny wagered a tenner.

Stikkan was very important to us at this point, as he paved the way with all his contacts in music and publishing and was, without a doubt, the driving force at that time. The eventual split between the group and Stikkan, due to a financial lawsuit that ABBA was forced to take out against him, and ultimately won, was a sad and sorry end to a successful collaboration.

Obviously, we'd seen what happened to Eurovision Song Contest winners, but to experience it ourselves was something else altogether. The champagne breakfast the next day, after just a few hours sleep, floated by in a rosy haze and we felt immense joy as we sat and read the masses of telegrams and good luck wishes that poured in.

We were driven at top speed in a Rolls-Royce up to London to appear on the television programme *Top Of The Pops* and swept along, in the same manner, to a world-wide career. To see everything that we'd worked for all those years suddenly become reality was bewildering and indescribable.

The euphoric Eurovision winners pose in Brighton the day after their victory.

THERE WAS A FEVER, THERE WERE OVATIONS

THERE WERE SWEATY, OBSESSED CROWDS

When the lights went down in the concert hall in Oslo, with Prince Harald and Princess Sonja seated in the front row, the rumbling of a helicopter could be heard in the dark.

The audience looked, questioningly, up toward the ceiling. When the noise reached a crescendo the spotlights were directed at the stage where ABBA, dressed in glowing white, stood captured by the beam of light. The cover of 'Arrival' – live.

In a show that lasted for one hundred minutes, the audience got all the hits they could ever wish to hear. ABBA generously offered up practically all of their songs, that are today classics, and they were hysterically received by an ecstatic audience.

ABBA with Prince Harald and Princess Sonja of Norway after the 1977 concert in Oslo.

ABBA audiences weren't the average pop crowd. ABBA are unique in having become popular with many generations simultaneously. There were parents with their teenage children, their younger brothers and sisters, and here and there a grandfather and grandmother.

ABBA were all they could wish for: two fresh, on the level, glamorous couples in love, who sang songs most of the people in the hall already knew off by heart.

It was the opening night of ABBA's 1977 world tour, which began in Oslo and ended in Australia. They were received everywhere in the same exceptional manner. In February they arrived in England, where they had dominated the charts for the entire previous year, for their first live performance. Demand for tickets was so high that it was said that they could have filled London's Royal Albert Hall a hundred times over.

Since the beginning of 1977 ABBA had an unbroken run of hits, with a small decline when 'Money, Money, Money' 'only' got to number three in the British charts. Innumerable awards swept over them. 'Arrival' was proclaimed the album of the year in the pop world and in the USA they were awarded their first gold disc.

Björn and Benny were carried along on a wave of creativity: applying greater content to the lyrics, greater substance to the music and the sound, they moved ever further from the usual, sugary pop songs and closer to a more artful role as songwriters/producers.

'Fernando' received an award for the year's best recording, and later in 1977 ABBA got another gold disc for the album 'Greatest Hits'.

Everything was crowned by Agnetha and Frida who elevated it all with their distinctive voices. 'Dancing Queen' went gold and was played around the world. They reached the top of the charts – from the Soviet Union to Australia,

A familiar ritual for ABBA and Stig 'Stikkan' Anderson.

from the USA to South Africa. Three million records were sold in that year alone.

In Sweden 'Dancing Queen' became especially associated with the Swedish Queen, ever since ABBA, dressed in fantastic rococo creations, sang it at the ball held when the royal couple married in 1976.

For the world tour Björn and Benny had written a mini-musical to be included in the show *The Girl With The Golden Hair*. Agnetha and Frida wore blonde wigs and dressed identically. The story was simple but contained many strong songs like 'I'm A Marionette', 'I Wonder' and, perhaps one of ABBA's greatest songs, 'Thank You For The Music', in which

Agnetha sang the melody with a mature, shimmering, multi-faceted voice.

The tour was extremely lavish and cost a fortune, so despite massive receipts and sold-out shows, profits were zero for ABBA according to Stikkan Anderson, but success was one hundred percent.

The second visit to Australia meant the terminal point of the world tour. However, neither they nor their retinue had much time to see any birds of paradise, expansive savannahs with bounding kangaroos, coral reefs, or steppes with wild horses on this grandiose continent, where there is an average of only two inhabitants per square kilometre and where, by that time, every other household owned an ABBA record.

One thing ABBA could verify was that they were already a hugely popular band in Australia. Perhaps it had never before been so clear to them, as here, just how big they had become.

As soon as they landed in their private jet, a 727, they were greeted by thousands of fans. Enormous crowds were attracted

Agnetha and Frida in the mini-musical The Girl With The Golden Hair.

to their concerts. They came from all corners of the country. At one venue over forty thousand people attended, whereupon ABBA decided to give two concerts instead of one, so that the risk of anyone being injured or trampled would be reduced. It had happened, tragically enough, to another band.

Agnetha was feted as a golden Nordic goddess, and it was also in Australia that a journalist cited her bottom as the sexiest in pop music. The press soon picked up on this and it has been frequently quoted ever since! Even if it irritated Agnetha, she took the opportunity to benefit from it and, laughing, often turned her back to the delighted audience

while she danced and sang in her tight, bright, satin costumes.

Björn and Agnetha had begun to plan for another child. To tie in with this, the idea came up of making a film and video. It was thought it might lower the fans' demands for live appearances for the while ahead.

The choice of producer and director was Lasse Hallstrom, who had made ABBA's publicity films. The film was called *ABBA – The Movie* and the documentary section of the film was recorded in Australia during early March 1977. It had an uncomplicated story line about a disc jockey at a radio station in Sydney, who had been given an assignment to do an in-depth interview with ABBA. He pursues the group all over Australia and after many days of fruitless attempts he finally gets face to face with them...

When *ABBA – The Movie* premiered in London in 1978, ABBA were present to receive 'Carl Allen's Song Writing Prize' from Princess Margaret in front of a sold-out house, with a large number of famous pop stars in the audience including Pete Townsend and Keith Moon of The Who. The film got more bad reviews than good but, none the less, by the end of the year it came closely behind *Star Wars*, *Grease* and *Saturday Night Fever* in ticket sales and, in fact, beat the popular film *Annie Hall*.

When the tour opened in Sydney a new ABBA frenzy broke out. Among other things, a crowd threatened to invade the stage in Melbourne.

The mechanics behind a successful phenomenon, like ABBA, that catches alight and then races across the world like a forest fire, are hard to grasp. Mass responses are not easily analysed or tamed.

Yes, the Australian tour was the most incredible of all the things that I experienced with ABBA. There was fever, there was hysteria, there were ovations, there were sweaty, obsessed crowds.

Sometimes it was awful. I felt as if they would get hold of me and I'd never get away again. It was as if I was going to be crushed. On occasions they would grab hold of us in the most unpleasant ways and there were times when we cried once we were inside the car.

No one who has experienced facing a screaming, boiling, hysterical crowd could avoid feeling shivers up and down their spine. It's a thin line between ecstatic celebration and menace. It can turn around in a flash.

I don't think anyone could stay the same after

such an encounter. It affects your personality. It remoulds you and can be the source of phobias. Naturally, it depends on how sensitive you are. Nonetheless I never felt that my life was in danger in Australia. Enthusiasm and warmth were always present too. We had a large security force of body guards and police around the clock, and always drove with the doors locked.

I was often worried that someone would get run over, when they threw themselves in front of the car or hurled themselves at it and began pounding on it. Sometimes it got frightening and we were forced to use excessive speed to get through the crowds.

The fans never left us alone and photographers were everywhere, even in the hotels. They were with us constantly. If we wanted to be alone we had to make secret plans, perhaps have a boat pick us up from a jetty somewhere.

So, there was a lot of pressure. Lasse Hallstrom's film crew also demanded a lot of our time and attention.

On the night of the première in Sydney, on the 3rd March, the city was hit by torrential rain. The rain hammered down and the open-air stage was covered in water. A huge crowd had gathered and, of course, you wondered if there would be a show for them at all.

We waited a long time for the rain to ease up. With so much electrical equipment around, guitars, microphones, sockets and so on, it made performing risky. However, we decided not to leave the soaking audience in the lurch, which was so much appreciated that we have probably never received such a rapturous reception anywhere – when we ran on to the stage it seemed the ovation would never end.

The stage was very slippery and at one point Frida fell over and really bumped herself. She quickly composed herself and we carried on without delay.

One thing I particularly noticed in Australia was that it makes no difference whether there are five thousand or fifty thousand in the crowd: I was still equally stressed and nervous. It seems the greater your success the greater the audiences' expectations and impatience, while at the same time you demand more and more of yourself.

The surrounding mechanism becomes incredibly complicated, with more and more people involved, people you never get time to know or even recognise. I imagine that it would be even worse to perform before small audiences in a little bar than in front of a big crowd. It is more intimate, revealing, almost like working in close-up the whole time – where every feature and expression is seen. When you're standing on stage in front of a huge sea of people, there's a certain anonymity. Obviously, what helped a lot was the assurance between the four of us, the musicians and everyone else on stage.

When we got back to Stockholm again the rest of *ABBA – The Movie* was recorded, on home turf.

I was expecting my second child, Christian, who was born on the 4th December, which was more important than anything else that happened to me in 1977.

ABBA'S LAST TOUR WAS A SUCCESS

BUT AWFUL FOR ME

The itinerary for the 1979 tour was massive and went by the grand title: 'ABBA North American and European Tour 1979.'

It was to be ABBA's last big tour – and perhaps the most trying of all – 35 cities covered with 45 concerts in 55 days.

The ABBA machine was well-oiled but required massive resources. There was a private jet for ABBA, a Jumbo jet for forty assistants and ABBA attendants (or 'The Poptrain' as it became known), thirty tons of equipment, four juggernauts, cars, buses and so on – a gigantic production.

This tour started in Canada, opening at the Edmonton Coliseum on 13 September, went through the USA's major cities, over to Scandinavia and on to Europe and, among other cities, Paris, Vienna, Munich, Frankfurt, then on to Brussels, ending in Dublin on 15 November.

Rehearsals had begun by May. Before that ABBA had made an important visit to the USA when the UN celebrated Year of the Child with a UNICEF gala in New York at the beginning of the year. They took part, as the only non-Anglo-Saxon group, along with other superstars like Rod Stewart, Olivia Newton-John, The Bee Gees, Kris Kristofferson & Rita Coolidge, Donna Summer and the actor Henry Fonda.

Each artist performed one song and donated the takings to UNICEF for all time. The gala was a peerless success and was broadcast first on American television and later most of the

world. ABBA sang 'Chiquitita', which made such a mark in South America amongst other places that they recorded it in Spanish. It became one of the most successful recordings ever released there.

Amid all this activity an important change had occurred within ABBA. Benny and Frida had married in the autumn of 1978 but Agnetha and Björn had decided to separate only a few months later, at Christmas 1978.

It had been an enormous metamorphosis from the happy, loving, euphoric quartet who had won in Brighton in 1974 with 'Waterloo', to the biggest pop/rock sensation of the 70s and 80s, a sophisticated group now falling apart from the inside on a personal level. There were many people who had thought Agnetha wouldn't take part in the massive tour, thereby splitting ABBA up, but she ignored all the dismaying rumours of catastrophe.

Before the divorce became official, ABBA had made yet another conquest – Japan, the world's second largest record market. Ten heavily booked days of television shows and live appearances had definitely opened up the nation to ABBA. Three of their albums were simultaneously in the Japanese top twenty.

On the way there they had also made a brief stop off in Hollywood, where their presence opportunely coincided with both 'Greatest Hits' and 'The Album' achieving platinum status in the USA.

Agnetha and Björn did their best to emphasise to the frenzied press that their's was an amicable divorce. There was no reason why ABBA should cease to be, they stated. How they felt inside was, naturally, another thing. Wounds had been opened and the things that had held them together now looked shaky. It took great self discipline for the pain not to show outwardly.

The USA is obviously an important market for all pop groups. Even for ABBA in 1979, with total sales worldwide of over fifty million copies. The first hit, 'Waterloo', had been followed by another fourteen hit singles and 'Dancing Queen' went in at number one in the American chart. 'The biggest record sales in the history of the record business' wasn't just a slogan for the publicity ballyhoo which flooded the USA in 1978, paving the way for the tour, but a fact.

ABBA had never toured in the USA, even if they had been seen fairly often on television. The public wasn't ready to believe in their existence until they had seen them live on stage! So, ABBA threw themselves into this tour, at breakneck

Six-year-old Linda Ulvaeus makes her stage debut with the children's choir at ABBA's 1979 concert in Las Vegas.

speed, with many dramatic moments. At one time their lives were jeopardised on a turbulent flight from New York to Boston.

For Agnetha a highlight of the tour was meeting up with Linda in Los Angeles and taking her to Las Vegas, the city that resembles a giant amusement park, the incarnation of luxurious entertainment, with frenetic games of chance and sensational shows at least twice nightly.

Even before leaving the airport you are bombarded by gaming machines. All visitors are hungry to play. On the main street, The Strip, huge hotels are tightly packed in next to each other. Neon advertising is so garish it lights up the entire sky at night. You can hardly differentiate between day and night. Even the revolving doors, leading into the luxury hotels, have dark glass in them and the arcades have no windows at all. You are not supposed to know what time of day it is but rather lose all sense of time so that gambling can go on 24 hours a day. If anywhere suits the song 'Money! Money! Money!' this is the place.

It wasn't the first time ABBA had been to Las Vegas. They had flown there before to record a television show. Now they were to have their own live show in front of the picky Las Vegas public, who were spoiled by superstars like Frank Sinatra and Liza Minelli.

Along The Strip are the most exclusive hotels such as The Sands, The Dunes, The Flamingo Hilton and The Aladdin where ABBA were going to perform in the huge red and gold theatre. The competition was tough, that same night Diana Ross was performing at Caesar's Palace and Engelbert Humperdink was at MGM.

The audience were very cold, hard to fire up, an unusual occurence for ABBA, who had otherwise been borne along on a wave of enthusiastic acclamation.

But then came a number that melted the hearts of the hard to please audience: 'I Have A Dream', which ABBA sang together with a twenty-strong children's choir.

No one in the audience knew that they were witnessing a stage debut. In the middle of the choir six-year-old Linda Ulvaeus was singing for all she was worth, while mum, Agnetha, knelt beside her and held her tightly.

Many female stars, with children, have probably had an experience similar to mine when ABBA took off. You are torn in two. One half is dying to succeed on the world stage, while the other half is a mother who wants to be at home taking care of her children.

Even though you are sucked into a career that's going at a dizzying pace, these two halves and all that they entail still have to be balanced. I, of course, had two children during the ten hectic ABBA years.

When Björn and I separated we always told the media that it was a 'happy' divorce, which, of course, was a front but also a way of saying that it was right for us and that we were in touch enough to deal with any problems that might arise. Obviously we all know that there is no such thing as a happy divorce. They are painful, especially when children are involved. On top of that it was in the full glare of the media.

It has always felt like a failure that Björn and I couldn't keep our family together. You never get it back, but to this day I don't regret splitting up. The reason behind our separation is one of those things I definitely don't want to go into.

Obviously I gave it a great deal of thought and tried to draw my own conclusions. They are not remarkable

but the sort of things anyone would arrive at; surely children need both a father and a mother and it's worth every effort to stay together and to take pains not to do anything too hasty. At least then you feel that 'we did our best' and have that to fall back on.

But there are marriages that turn out to be destructive and then there's no going back.

My desire, during the ABBA years, to keep my career and the children separate means that I've come in for a lot of criticism and appeared to be the one who upset the apple cart by 'fussing' about wanting sufficient time at home. I had definite conditions that tours in far climes should not last more than two or three weeks at a time, and did everything I could to demand them. But it didn't work.

Linda and Christian were so vulnerable as celebrity children that I wanted to be there as much as possible for them and try to be a good role model. I have, for example, expressly distanced myself from drugs throughout the years and have made that quite clear in interviews. I find it unacceptable that there have been so many drug-related deaths among kids, and have tried to be informed enough to give my children the facts. I've really tried to make them aware of the pitfalls.

A lot of people believe that generally I don't have a social conscience, just because I don't advertise my beliefs and ideas and don't express an opinion on every situation. I'm not exactly one to stand on the barricades. But that doesn't mean that I don't do anything at all. I work behind the scenes and donate money to many different causes. It feels good to do it. Sometimes I think I would like to do much more.

When I chose to put the children first it wasn't to escape to a cosy, safe little world. I tried to follow my heart and take responsibility for their lives, to see that they would get to grow up in conditions as normal as possible, with a secure place in a world where they were often caught in the spotlight because of their parents' fame. From the moment that they were born they have been exposed to press curiosity.

On the whole, I have taken the main responsibility for Linda and Christian. Once Björn had moved to London and the divorce had gone through I strongly felt that I was the children's only security. I was also grateful to be able to make good the time I had lost during the ABBA years. At the same time I felt terribly worried, not about failing, but that I wouldn't quite be able to cope or perhaps miss out on something because I was single.

However, you really aren't complete as a woman just because you have a man by your side. Solitude can also be extremely stimulating. You feel a sense of liberty and are especially sensitive to outside ideas. You're so vulnerable in one way and incredibly strong in another. You develop as a person and learn to tackle so much more than you thought you could. Even practical things like battling with the boiler, the pool units and suchlike. So you become what you become: an independent woman.

I hadn't reached that level of maturity when we began the USA tour of 1979, which turned out to be ABBA's last big tour together. It was momentous and successful but for me it was awful. Björn and I had separated and I had torn myself away from the children. I just wanted to be home, home, home.

But I had no choice. Björn and I were agreed about doing this tour together, despite the divorce, so we had

'ABBA's success out on the road was inconceivably massive. Australia, England, USA, Japan, Sweden – we were acclaimed everywhere.'

to form a new relationship with each other and work together in a new way. It was an unfamiliar situation for all four of us – an ordeal by fire. I had no one to talk to. So I mourned alone. The whole time I ached inside for the children and from home sickness.

Today, I don't know how I managed. The other couple were in a different phase and managed better. They didn't have children at home who had just gone through their parents' divorce. It was me who had to live with a constant bad conscience. No one understood how painful it was. It's still difficult to talk about it. I got through the tour, though, and it was very successful.

So, talk of me ending ABBA's career is wrong. Where has that rumour come from and why does it continue to circulate?

This had nothing to do with the public, they were wonderful. For me touring was about everything I didn't like; too long away from the children, long journeys, changing hotels every day, time changes. Perhaps just because the whole thing was so hard, the audiences' enthusiastic reception was a fantastic contrast and an indescribable joy.

The moments when the songs, the orchestra and the audience are totally absorbed by the music are wonderful and make all the hard work and innumerable concerts in strange towns in different continents worthwhile. You forget your ego and go into another state. You convey something of yourself but the audience also gives a lot in return.

As an artist you are very sensitive to the public's responses. There are wonderful moments when the air is suddenly electric. I remember a few of those golden moments. I fell ill during the 1979 tour and the Washington concert had to be postponed. There were only two concerts left in Canada – Montreal and Toronto. I wanted to show up, at any price, for the public there although my legs were unsteady. They also showed up for me and that carried me through. When twelve thousand people in Montreal get up and wave and applaud a wave of energy hits you. You are given strength and are rewarded for all the hard work and it feels fantastic.

ABBA's success out on the road was inconceivably massive. Australia, England, USA, Japan, Sweden – we were acclaimed everywhere.

What unbelievable contrasts between our first show, 'Festfolket', in Gothenburg and Stockholm, when hardly anyone at all came to the opening night, and everything we subsequently experienced around the world. Every concert was like a party once the nerves had settled. As soon as we were on stage it became playful, we joked with each other and the musicians, thought up practical jokes, played off one another and thought it was great when something unexpected happened.

You become very close-knit in a band when you're out travelling, and develop a special humour and jargon between you. The press were a little surprised that we didn't have bigger rave-ups than we did, but instead could often be found jogging and exercising. No doubt we had a clean cut image, but we did have a few wild times on the road.

There are so many memories. The concerts at the Albert Hall in England were unforgettable. The English were crazy about us. The Albert Hall was sold out a long way in advance and we could easily have stayed and packed it out for weeks.

When the concerts began it was ecstatic. After the opening number, when both we and the audience had calmed down, it was great when the tempo got its second wind. Some magic moments ensued. A concert that is especially close to my heart was at home in Sweden, in Gothenburg. Apart from anything else it received very good reviews and the wonderful atmosphere continued in Stockholm, where we performed next.

I had my own number called 'I'm Still Alive'. It was never recorded, but we always played it in concert. It was a ballad, so the audience would be nice and quiet. I sat at the piano and played and sang. Suddenly, when the lights went down, little by little small lights came on in the dark. People had brought lighters with them and soon there would be a sea of shimmering flames which flickered everywhere. We all became spellbound, the magic of music was so palpable. It was one of my greatest moments.

ABBA – into the eighties and coming the to the end of a stunning career together.

WE HAD REACHED A DIVIDING LINE

IT WAS TIME FOR EVERYONE TO GO THEIR OWN WAY

Agnetha began 1983 staring at newspaper placards that went up in Sweden on 23 January and then resounded around the world.

The article, in *Dagens Nyheter*'s Sunday edition, was a big spread. Something of a bomb had dropped in the pop world. What everyone had speculated about – the break up of ABBA – was there in black and white. There were many people who choked on their morning coffee.

Only three days earlier she had begun recording 'Wrap Your Arms Around Me', her first solo LP in English, at Polar Studios in Stockholm. During her time with ABBA she had become familiar with having big-selling hits and learned the special art of collaboration. Now she was going to stand alone on stage again in front of a partially new audience, and everything was down to her.

Agnetha was in fine form, fresh and resolute. She gets a kick from challenges, the bigger the better. They stimulate her. She blossoms and gets a twinkle in her eye. The easily-bored air she can reveal during routine days disappears.

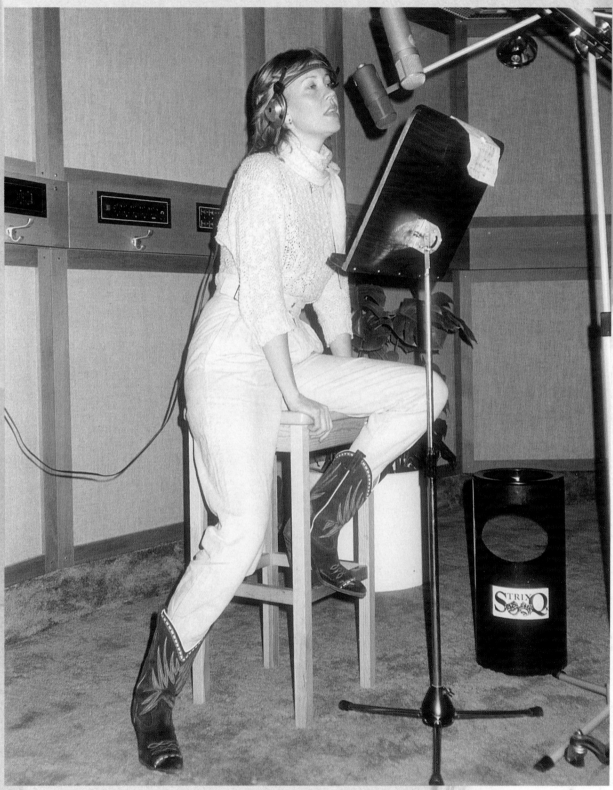

Agnetha pursues her solo career.

In the studio with producer Mike Chapman.

Australian-born Mike Chapman was producer of the LP, and together with Holly Knight had written the title track. The veteran Micke Tretow who'd been at all of ABBA's recordings was in place, top musicians were hired, and Sveriges Radio Symphony Orchestra provided the strings.

Agnetha and the record company had thought deeply before they chose Mike Chapman. She felt that he was a safe bet, having had a lot of experience as one half, with Nicky Chinn, of Chinnichap. He had written and produced a number of hits during the 70s for Mud, Suzi Quatro, Sweet and Smokie.

On 20 January recording began. For the first track on side one, Palmer and Ashton's fiery song 'The Heat Is On' was chosen.

When the LP came out it was a hit all over Europe. Mike was a pragmatic record producer who almost always took Agnetha's suggestions on board. Her ideas were good and original. The pair had a similar, well-developed, ear for nuance.

Agnetha worked solidly, scrupulous to the point of pedantry. She listened and learned. She already had experience as a producer so she knew the techniques. She sat, perched on a high stool, with earphones on. When she came in on the music she sang with a powerful intensity and sensitivity. She knew exactly when a take was right.

The final leg of 'Wrap Your Arms Around Me' went at a burning pace, over fifteen hours work a day, every day.

Up in the morning at 7 o'clock so that Linda could get off to school and Christian to nursery school, a fully charged day's work then home again, to Lidingo, in the evening to take care of routine things and tuck the children up. Sometimes they fell ill and that meant sitting up at nights. It doesn't help when mother is a world famous star.

With ABBA, the intense tempo wasn't something that Agnetha had control over, but at least she did when it came to producing and promoting her first solo LP. Somewhat. An LP is always a hectic business, however well-planned it all is, but at least she was working on home turf.

'Wrap Your Arms Around Me' came out first in Sweden, in May 1983, then in the USA and the rest of the world. In the first year alone it sold 1.2 million copies, and paved the way for Agnetha's next big projects, 'Eyes Of A Woman' and 'I Stand Alone'.

Now, when I look back on 1983 I see what an amazing year it was in many ways. A huge upheaval and a lot of drama. The end of ABBA, my first film part, my first solo album after ABBA, PR journeys abroad and my first self-owned production company.

Dagens Nyheter's headline in January, which caused such a big stir, wasn't news to ABBA. We had always had an unspoken agreement between us: when it no longer seems fun we'll call it a day.

Björn and Benny had shelved the next project, 'Opus 10', to write the musical *Chess* with Tim Rice, the man behind *Jesus Christ Superstar*. Frida had moved abroad. We had reached a dividing line. We felt pretty tired of ABBA and everything surrounding it. It was time for all of us to go our separate ways, so that we could concentrate on our individual careers, so that we could grow. It was a natural progression.

Personally, I thought it felt good to work on my own stuff again, to try new directions. It just happened to be me that broke the news in the *Dagens Nyheter* interview. Neither Björn, Benny nor Frida responded to the headlines. But across the country and around the world it led to a torrent of questions. Was it just a temporary

break? Would ABBA ever make a new record together or had it come to a complete standstill on that front? How long would it be? Did we have any tours planned, any other projects under way?

We couldn't answer the questions ourselves, because none of us knew. Whether our paths crossed again depended on how we all developed. Perhaps, in the back of our minds, we thought that if Björn and Benny did any suitable songs we might work together again.

I didn't really understand, when I gave the interview to Brita Åhman, just how big a step it was, that it was actually the end of ABBA. At least it seems so today. I knew inside that I definitely never wanted to work at the high tempo that ABBA had, again. All the tours, film and television recordings, long tiring journeys, gala appearances, reaching out to the world in front of hundreds of thousands of fans – and the children left at home.

The whole time I had been forced to make my work a priority. However, after the divorce from Björn and the big tour of 1979 I reached a point when I decided that now the children must come first. Nothing was more important. My intention was to never be away from them for such long periods again. The situation had changed, Björn had moved to London so I, alone, was responsible for them.

When I started to work on my own again it was fun to be able to go for it in a new way. When you work with a group you have to think about everyone else all the time, and how to make room for their individual charisma. At the same time I felt a bit isolated. I saw how protected we'd been by the extra security you get on stage when a number of you perform together. Although

it was still lovely to be there on my own again. I had gained so much experience and could now freely use it as I wished.

I experienced roughly the same mixed feelings of delight and vulnerability when I made the film *Raskenstam* with Gunnar Hellstrom, but really I think it just stimulated me. I was very motivated and have always been fascinated by film. Gunnar was both producer and male lead. The collaboration with him went very well. His time in Hollywood had made him very professional and provided him with a wealth of experience. He also had a fine sense of humour and we complemented each other very well. Actually we'd considered making another film together, but when there was talk of a sequel to *Raskenstam* I wasn't at all enthusiastic about the suggestion. This idea of trying to repeat a success doesn't interest me. It's only really done to make more money.

When I started my new solo LP, demand was sky high and expectations great. People had been listening to ABBA for ten years and Frida had released an LP. Now it was my turn. The whole world waited for my solo LP, that was how it seemed. Obviously I felt the pressure. It made me hesitant about approving some of the songs I'd done, which, perhaps, really were good enough. There is a danger of changing too much in the search for perfection.

Today, when I hear my last three LPs after ABBA I'm no longer pleased by them. It's a fact that when you're in the middle of working on a new record you think it's fantastically good. Perhaps it's instinctive to feel like that so that you manage to finish it. You give it your all and believe that the recordings are better than they are. When I listen to them now I sometimes wonder why on earth we did certain songs. A lot of them don't feel nearly as good as they did then.

It's probably the first LP, 'Wrap Your Arms Around Me', that I feel best about and from that I like 'The Heat Is On' most of all. It felt powerful from the beginning.

WHEN I'M ACTING OUT A LIFE

IN THE WORLD OF LUXURY AND CELEBRITY, IT'S A WALK-ON PART NOT A VITAL NECESSITY

The promotion of 'Wrap Your Arms Around Me' involved trips abroad to the USA, Paris, Milan and London. When it was finished, Agnetha had done seventeen television programmes, twenty-eight radio interviews and over a hundred newspaper interviews.

She took the Orient Express from Milan to London. Before that she had been in Paris, where she had caught a heavy cold. Her throat closed up and she had a high fever. It couldn't have been worse, what with the pre-booked live transmissions on television and radio, interviews and meetings with record company representatives and invitations of all kinds.

After dinner at a small Parisian restaurant she opted for an all-or-nothing cure of antibiotics. She would have preferred to go to bed and be looked after, but that wasn't going to happen.

'My strength in an artist's world is being anchored by the children.' Agnetha with her son Christian during a rehearsal.

Despite being ill her shows in Paris and Milan went well. In both cities she got a positive response from audiences on live television. In Paris she sang 'The Heat Is On' and in the middle of the song received storming applause. The same thing happened in Milan, during three television broadcasts, where she sang 'I Can't Shake Loose' and 'Wrap Your Arms Around Me'. At the beginning of the 1980s such audience reactions were unusual on live television.

The journey on the venerable old Orient Express wasn't the relaxation Agnetha had hoped for, even if she did think that the train was beautiful and impressive. The Orient Express, which had once started from Constantinople, (now Istanbul), had been out of service for decades but had come back into existence on the initiative of the multi-millionaire James Sherwood. He had the romantic and expensive idea of rebuilding it and letting it roll anew.

Agnetha took the Paris – London stage, for the last part of her PR trip to London. Enviable, thought many. Awful, thought Agnetha when, four hours late and stressed out before pre-booked engagements that day, she arrived at Victoria Station. The train had been standing for two hours in the Simplon tunnel, which cuts through Monte Leone in the Alps. Her tour manager and her director of PR had become hardened to such things, but she had almost fallen out of bed several times in the night due to some very sharp breaking .

'You should take the Orient Express only if you've got plenty of time, haven't got any work waiting for you and are a couple who don't have any great urge to sleep,' she exclaimed, when she stepped off the train in London.

It's fun to be successful, but you can't enjoy it if you're ill. So despite the warm reception I got everywhere during my travels it still felt excruciating to work under so much pressure, when I wasn't on top form. I knew that I had so much more to give, but it doesn't really come naturally when you're not well. You have to battle to get on. My professional persona never loosens its grip, keeping an eye on me at all times. I continued, even though I knew I should have stopped.

At the end of the tour I felt very tired, mentally. I often do more than I should and it's only me that suffers. It's been like that ever since I was fifteen, when I first began to sing for real. I may have aimed too high sometimes, asked too much of myself and demanded too little from those around me.

Obviously you don't reach the top without paying a price. In a way you sacrifice yourself. For what? For the public? For money? I don't know. In any case it's always been important for me to fulfil my plans. But I seriously started to mull a few things over during this tour. Not that I have regretted my choices, but I did ask myself what the underlying meaning of it all was.

I often get praise, and that pleases me, but after a while I have to analyse everything I've achieved. I can spot empty flattery and know exactly where I stand. In the end it's really only my own approval or disapproval that means anything. I don't care to make excuses if something goes wrong and have no problem taking the blame, even if I wasn't the cause.

Perhaps sometimes my tolerance can appear boundless, but it does have its limits. If someone goes too far I can get furious. Perhaps I've stretched my tolerance too far and kept my feelings bottled up for too long.

My strength in an artist's world is being anchored by the children, the home, the family and my own common sense. When I'm living in the world of luxury and celebrity, which is where I've found myself for a large part of my life, it's a walk-on part. Not a vital necessity, like it is for so many people. I enjoy it but I can see right through it.

It's at home with the family and a few other people, true friends from outside showbiz glamour, where my real life is led. It's that which keeps me going through the pop world's exhibitionism, appearances in front of enormous, often hysterical crowds and through parties where people drink copiously and only talk about themselves or whatever bolsters their egos. How many similar events I've been to! They never lead to anything!

The attention Agnetha got in London surpassed everything else on the trip. The red double-deckers slammed on their brakes so that people could catch a better glimpse of her. When she walked past a delicatessen the entire window was suddenly full of waving, laughing cooks in high white chef's hats. Whenever she went out shopping there were photographers constantly on her heels. Then there were the fans, of course. At a lunch bar she'd impulsively popped into for a bite to eat there was a queue at her table. They wanted autographs for themselves, friends, brothers and sisters and cousins.

Megastars often have a large entourage on their travels, just as royalty and presidents travel with a retinue. ABBA had it in their day.

Personally, Agnetha took three people with her on her PR trips in 1983; Marie Ledin, director of PR, Hasse Blomgren, tour manager and Lolo Murray, make-up, hair and clothing. Earlier they had been on ABBA's tours. Naturally there were additional people in each city that they visited. Every day

they met for breakfast in Agnetha's hotel suite at The Dorchester. A big table was wheeled in to the suite's roomy lounge which functioned as the meeting area.

One morning a bundle of newspapers had arrived from Sweden. In one of the weeklies there was an all too well-informed article about very personal details of Agnetha's private life, which only a few close people could have known. It was apparent that someone had leaked the information. Suddenly the atmosphere in the beautiful lounge changed. Different theories on how the details could have got out were put forward. Telephone bugging? Had 'the outer circle' which was close to 'the inner circle' been responsible? In which case the trusted inner circle hadn't kept quiet. People squabbled. Everybody was badly affected. Not least Agnetha herself.

Despite her assurances that she didn't suspect anyone present, everyone was very disturbed and felt an instinctive need to defend themselves. Obviously, it was pointless discussing the matter because no one was going to own up.

For Agnetha these episodes are equally unpleasant every time they happen. However, it is next to impossible to trace a leak. The people around a big artist always swear loyalty and friendship. Yet the person you least suspect can be the one to disappoint you.

Superstars have to learn to live with this uncertainty. It is a universal problem for all artists. In this respect their world, though securely cemented by riches and success, is remarkably frail. Everybody wants to join in worshipping the Golden Calf but how many are left if success disappears or the money runs out? Often none at all.

'I probably won't get away from this sort of thing until I get out of the business,' said Agnetha, with a sigh. That, at any rate, was what she thought then. Little did she know what was to come.

WHAT'S YOUR FAVOURITE COLOUR?

WHAT DO YOU DO ON AN ORDINARY SUNDAY?
HAVE YOU GOT ANY PETS?
WHO'S THE MAN IN YOUR LIFE?

The Dorchester is one of London's most famous hotels. Most celebrities, of any significance, have stayed there in the past. To sit at a table in The Promenade at tea time, or during the cocktail hour, is like finding yourself in the middle of a film sequence.

Agnetha moves naturally and without any overtones in this milieu. But she knows that she attracts attention. All eyes turn towards her as she walks through the revolving door at the entrance, especially the men's. Of all ages.

When she returned from the broadcast of *Top of the Pops* she was happy and relaxed. She looked exquisite in a chalk-white long coat, black leather trousers, black top, pumps and a trendy haircut. Her eyes shone deep blue. Dinner afterwards was a relaxed affair at the fashionable restaurant Wheeler's, with fresh asparagus, grilled lobster, a chilled Chablis and wild strawberries and ice cream for dessert. Agnetha was on top form. Rehearsals and television recordings had gone like clockwork.

In the middle of the main course some fans popped up who wanted autographs. No problem. Unembarrassed, they sat down at her table and took their time with their idol. The guests gorged themselves while Agnetha's food went cold.

The next day the press had been booked for interviews. In London, the first one in a whole series, began with the fascinating question 'What do you eat for breakfast?'

'Well, I start with a few glasses of pink champagne.' retorted Agnetha quickly.

The reporter took her answer seriously and it took a while to straighten things out. He carried on with a stream of equally interesting questions: What's your favourite colour? What do you do on an ordinary Sunday? Have you got any pets? Who is the man in your life after the divorce from Björn? Nothing about the songs, the music, the tour or the challenge of standing alone on stage without ABBA after ten years with the world-famous pop group, or anything about her plans for the future. Interviews like that are almost impossible to get through without some initiative from the interviewee.

After a number of interviews with similar questions Agnetha started giving routine, insignificant replies. She has answered the same questions hundreds of times. In the end she just gets bored. However, if she gets interesting questions that catch her attention she is prepared to answer in depth and gives some surprising replies.

It happened once when she showed up for an interview with one of England's worst tabloids, digging for 'the truth behind ABBA'. At one point she was close to ending it and walking out. Then she got a stubborn gleam in her eye, which she often gets in tricky situations.

She went through every question scrupulously. Gave the facts. Cut out any ambiguity. Came to grips with the journalist, posed counter questions. Suddenly the reporter was captivated and went back to the fun questions. What might have been a catastrophe became something constructive. At the end of the interview there was no doubt about who had been victorious in the duel. Both of them. The article, which went to press that night, was unusually flattering and considerate.

Out shopping in London.

ALL THE YEARS ON STAGE

HAVE GIVEN ME A ROUTINE AND DISCIPLINE WHICH HELPS WHEN SOMETHING UNEXPECTED HAPPENS...

Every live transmission on television puts an enormous strain on everyone involved: the anchorman and the stars, all the technicians from sound, light and camera to the producer, scriptwriter, floor manager and sound supervisor. Everything has to work to within tenths of a second.

Nerves are on tenterhooks, too much so for some people. Nothing is insignificant. Everything must work.

The audience on live television is important; they feel it too. On anchorman Noel Edmonds' extraordinarily popular *Late, Late Breakfast Show*, which was broadcast at 6.15 p.m. every Saturday during 1983, the audience were clearly conscious of their importance, and really in the swing of things. The consummate floor manager worked them up higher and higher before the show began.

This was Agnetha's last job in London and perhaps the most important of the tour. She had been personally invited on to the show by Edmonds, with whom she'd worked before. Agnetha was the special guest. She was going to perform and be presented with an award, 'The Golden Egg', for the blunder of the year, chosen from out-takes of film and television recordings in which someone had made a fool of themselves. The film clip Agnetha was getting her award for was from Gunnar Hellstrom's *Raskenstam*: Lisa/Agnetha is going to show her new baby to the father Raskenstam/Hellstrom, who is in hospital.

Instead of a baby she has a teddy bear, well wrapped up in a blanket, in her arms.

'Look how like you he is,' says Lisa to Raskenstam whereupon they both dissolve into hysterics. The scene had to be reshot many times. In the end they manage to keep straight faces and Lisa climbs into bed with Raskenstam.

'Oh, my God, I've still got my hat on!' she cries. She had: a little grey hat, with a pretty blue feather, was still sitting on her head.

The rehearsals had gone well and the programme was about to go out on BBC1. The audience were at boiling point when transmission began. During a pre-recorded segment, which featured various clips of Agnetha and ABBA, Agnetha got ready to make her entrance. The floor manager was going to give her precise directions. First, off camera, she would climb some stairs and then, on a given signal, come down

another staircase on camera and walk across the stage to be interviewed by Noel Edmonds beside a podium, where she would receive her award. Finally she would mime *I Can't Shake Loose* to a recorded playback. Suddenly, they notice how pressed for time they are, so she rushes up the stairs to get in to position.

But it all happens too quickly and she is forced to stop abruptly. Just as Edmonds announces her there is a crashing sound. From the audience's perspective you can see a pair of slender legs and two snake-skin court shoes sticking up in the air. On camera all that can be seen is Noel Edmonds' perplexed face. He was completely nonplussed. Everybody seemed paralysed. What had happened? Had Agnetha injured herself? Would they have to cut the live transmission?

Despite being hurt Agnetha made a fantastic entrance, laughing and maintaining her composure. The audience laughed too because they thought it was all an example of her sense of humour; that she had planned a little surprise of her own for Noel. She didn't let on that she had injured her arm and back in the fall. Quickly she latched on to the humour in the situation; she had come on the show to get first prize for the best blunder and then she tumbles over backwards making her entrance.

'Now I've arranged two blunders instead of one' she said calmly to the horror-stricken Noel Edmonds.

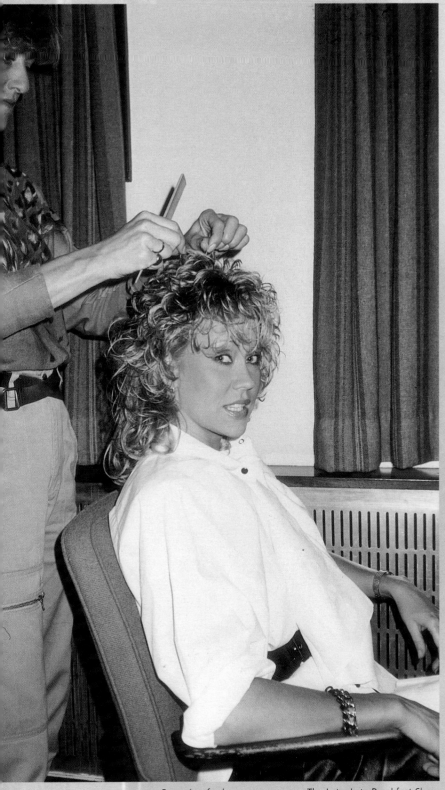

Preparing for her appearance on The Late, Late Breakfast Show.

When the floor manager missed my cue I stressed out going up the stairs and got there too soon. Quickly I took a step back so as not to be seen. But there was nothing there! I fell backwards headlong into a hole in the specially built stairs. I lay there, unable to get up while I listened to the live announcement: 'Tonight's special guest and award winner, Agnetha Fältskog.'

The seconds flew by. I was fully aware of what it meant if I didn't get up in a hurry. Noel would be forced to say that there'd been an accident and rearrange the running order of the programme, possibly abandon the whole thing. There would be a big hullabaloo, because what could they do instead? The show had been arranged around my appearance.

It felt like an eternity before anyone came to my assistance and gave me a push from behind so that I could get back up. My legs were trembling and my hands were shaking. Three fatal errors in one programme! The floor manager who simply mustn't miss the main guest's cue, badly built scenery which could have resulted in a serious accident, and my own fall backwards.

As I lay in the hollow I remember thinking that if I can just get up I'll save the show and carry through what I've come to London for. After all, it would have been awful if, after three PR trips and seventeen television programmes, I hadn't made it. During all my years on stage, since I was fifteen, and all the trips around the world with ABBA, nothing like this had ever happened. Imagine, we've been in so many dangerous situations and given performances on risky outdoor stages when the rain has poured down and there was imminent danger of electric shocks.

During one of our tours I had to run up a steel staircase on to a really high platform and sing 'Gimme ! Gimme ! Gimme !' Up, quickly, in high heels to sing a solo verse then race back down again and join in on the rest of the song with the others. It was very unpleasant, especially when I had to rush down the slippery steps, but it was always alright.

Of course, a few hilarious things happened like someone forgetting the words, dropping things or gadgets breaking down.

In Australia when we went on the road with 'The Girl With The Golden Hair', Frida and I were wearing identical blonde wigs. Under them our hair was held up with stockings and right at the top a tuft of hair poked out. Suddenly, during a dance sequence Frida's wig came off and the stocking and the whole lot was caught in the spotlight. Frida didn't lose her composure but quickly grabbed her wig and placed it back on top of her head.

These things happened, now and again, but they were mere trifles compared to what happened to me on *The Late, Late Breakfast Show*. On that occasion there were factors involved beyond my control.

All the years with ABBA have given me a routine and discipline which helps when something unexpected happens. In showbiz you are constantly trained to concentrate your abilities on the short span of a performance, while other people can spread theirs out between nine and five.

It was fortunate that the song was pre-recorded playback because I think I would rather have stayed in that hole than have had to sing live!

I REMEMBER THE LAST AWFUL THUMP

WHEN WE OVERTURNED AND SPAN AROUND

I have travelled all over the world. The sort of thing most people dream of doing. But the many journeys meant something completely different to me than they would to most people. They weren't associated with experiences of nature, smells, unusual incidents, unexpected exciting meetings and the interesting and intimate talks that can arise with the person sitting next to you on a plane ten thousand feet above the ground.

It was just hard, hard work, high tempo, a strain on the nerves, arduous schedules, performance demands, thousands of fans' enthusiastic but often pushy attentiveness and inescapable pathetic after-show parties.

Superficially the travelling was fantastic: of course we always flew first class, we were picked up in dark-windowed limousines, stayed at the poshest hotels with their exceptional suites: marble bathrooms as big as an ordinary one-room apartment, well-stocked bars and dazzling flower arrangements. However, once you were actually there in the extravagant luxury suite, you were usually so exhausted, from working and meeting and talking to all the people after the concert, that you couldn't enjoy the luxury. You were often smothered in well-meaning flattery which left a sort of vague empty feeling.

There was seldom time to experience the country or city you were in, to go out and get a feeling for the place, see the sights or enjoy the music or culinary culture. What you saw were airports, television and radio stations, the room you gave your interviews in and concert arenas. We didn't actually cancel a single press conference during our ten years in ABBA, and only two concerts.

When I went shopping it was mostly for new stage costumes or presents for the children. Sometimes I'd find something nice that looked good on me and then I did take pleasure in not having to look at the price tag.

When the PR trip for 'Wrap Your Arms Around Me' was done I was travelling from London home to Sweden in a specially outfitted tour bus. Ever since I was involved in a horrendous near accident on a flight, during ABBA's 1979 tour of the USA, I've been uneasy about flying. Our small private jet got caught in a violent thunderstorm and hurricane strength winds. The fuel gauge raced towards empty and the airport we were supposed to land at had blown down. I was convinced that we were going to crash but at the last minute the pilots managed to set us down.

Anyone who has experienced anything like it knows what terror means. Even if you force yourself to fly again it stays with you, if the incident was awful enough. Since then I've avoided flying where possible. People have often had a go at me about it.

I've tried to get over it but haven't managed it yet. Unfortunately I've always felt discomfort before flights, despite all the favourable statistics and the safety procedures they have. I have solved the problem, quite simply, by taking buses, cars, trains or boats. I'd

travelled that way during the PR trips of 1983. Except to the USA, of course, when I flew.

Late on the night of 1 October the entire tour crew ate supper in my suite, after my last television show, on the BBC. Everyone joked, toasted and talked all at once, relieved that the tour had been a success and that only the journey home remained.

At the last moment we decided that Brita Åhman, who'd been with us in London, wouldn't fly home as planned but instead take the bus with me. After supper I was really happy when we stepped on to the bus outside The Dorchester. At last, I was going home, having completed what I'd set out to do.

The bus was superbly fitted out, with a television and video, a fridge full of delicacies and masses of flowers, sweets and fruit, on board. Right at the back Brita and I each had our own sleeping compartments, with comfortable beds. Two drivers took it in turns driving. We felt safe and well looked after. Imagine, what a cosy way of travelling from port to port.

The ferry over to Calais and the journey up through Germany and Denmark went without a hitch. On the evening of 2 October we drove in to Skane. It was dark, rainy and the mist was thick on the Skane flatlands. Nevertheless, I thought it was great to be in Sweden again and was anticipating coming up to my childhood home town of Jonkoping. We were going to eat dinner there and I could have a long undisturbed chat on the telephone with the children, who were at their father's in England.

I had laid down for a while to rest before dinner and was flicking through a few weeklies we'd bought in Sweden. I was pleased to find, there were only positive

At the Groucho Club, London.

stories about me; in fact not even the tiniest cock-and-bull story.

Just then there was a smash.

The bus began to career violently from side to side. There was a squeal of brakes and raised voices. I was thrown around and hit myself hard on the head and legs. They were grave moments when I first realised that we were having an accident. I didn't see anything because I was back in the sleeping compartment. But I do remember the last awful thump when we overturned and span around and the crashing of glass.

I grabbed hold of the mattress that I'd been lying on and instinctively curled up into a ball to protect my face. Then it all went black.

I came to in a ditch. I had been hurled through the back window of the bus like a projectile. Amazingly enough the mattress had protected me. Without it I would surely have been cut to pieces – or maybe dead.

'Thank the Lord I'm alive,' was my first thought. Then I heard Brita's voice calling my name over and over again, but I couldn't reply. I was struck dumb. At once, when I heard her voice, I realised that she had survived.

At that moment I discovered that the bus lay at a precarious angle above me. I thought that it was going to tip over on to me. There was smoke coming from it, too.

I realised that the danger of an explosion was imminent. So I dug my nails into the ground, got to my feet and made my way up to the motorway. I saw the others there. I'll never forget that moment, when we all stood in a trembling circle and held each other, unable to say a word, grateful that we'd made it.

The driver had been going too fast. When he came to some road works and the lights were red he slammed on the brakes. The back wheels locked. A lorry had leaked oil at the lights, so it was slick for two reasons: rain and oil. So the bus skidded inexorably towards the oncoming traffic. We missed a lorry by a hair's breadth, span around once and turned over with great force.

Only a few metres away was a high viaduct. If the accident had happened there we would have crashed straight through the railings and down on to the road below.

We were taken care of by a friendly old lady from a little house by the roadside. Fire engines, breakdown trucks and ambulances were called out and soon arrived.

'If you believe in miracles then this is a good example,' one of the rescue crew had said. No one could comprehend how we had survived when they saw the wrecked, overturned, smoking bus, with its wheels stuck in the air. The ambulance crew were absolutely wonderful, impressive, professional and calm. They had a kind of gallows humour which was incredibly salutary and toned down the awfulness of it all.

The driver and tour manager had come out of it with minor injuries, but Brita and I were driven at top speed to Emergency at Angelholm's general hospital, where we were received by a rather arrogant young doctor who bestowed upon us the least possible solicitude.

The rest of the hospital staff did a fine job, but the photographers' hunt for us, even within the hospital walls was nasty. I wasn't too surprised when I was taken down to the X-ray department and was met by a newspaper photographer, rather than the doctor in charge of X-rays. I had to quickly pull the sheet over my head while the nurses stood protectively around me.

News of the accident was all over the country and had even gone international. The switchboard and the hospital entrance were blocked by journalists and photographers. Disconsolate doctors came and asked me what they should do. As if I could help them in my state of shock! We spent that night in the intensive care unit. I couldn't help repeating, over and over again, how wonderful it was that all five people on the bus had survived with their lives intact.

And I had to laugh while I lay there picking glass splinters out of my hair and arms. It was both absurd and screamingly funny thinking about what had happened in London during *The Late, Late Breakfast Show.*

It's said that a person shows their true colours in crisis situations. Personally I can be very calm at the time but cry and be very jittery afterwards. Fortunately, I can also see the funny side of certain situations. That makes things easier.

The doctor only gave us a certificate of illness for a week despite concussion and other fairly serious injuries that weren't clearly diagnosed. As early as the next morning we were discharged home to Stockholm without any briefing or advice.

So, there we were, in a limo, shocked, pallid and shaky, with aching heads and out in traffic once again. I had a neck brace on because of a muscle strain I'd received when I was thrown through the bus window. I was very meditative. The bus crash was undoubtedly another hurdle to get over. Was I now going to be afraid of being in cars as well? However, quite soon after

getting back home I sat myself down behind the wheel and drove. No problems.

Of course I was met by an enormous crowd of photographers when I arrived home in Lidingo. Afterwards the newspaper headlines were no longer sympathetic. They were as dark as night. The accident, with pictures of the overturned bus, dominated newspaper placards. According to the weeklies and their own little soap opera about me I was no longer pregnant.

Allegedly, I'd had a miscarriage!

IT HAD BECOME A GUT REACTION OF MINE

TO PROTECT MYSELF FROM THE PRESS

When the press compare Greta Garbo and Agnetha Fältskog and call Agnetha our new Garbo it is well-founded only with regard to their shyness and loathing of the media.

The relentless pursuit has led to their doing everything they can to protect their private lives. They have had an intense need for seclusion and in that sense they are kindred spirits.

Garbo considered that everything written about her in newspapers was made up, giving a false picture of her. At one point she said, 'I never speak to the press, so how can they know anything about me?'

When you read Greta Garbo's letters or some of the few interviews she gave, you can also see a number of other similarities with Agnetha. The disgust for superficial and empty celebrity parties, underlining their yearning for propinquity and simplicity. The uneasiness about people, fear of crowds. The long walks, often alone, in the countryside irrespective of bleak weather or stormy sea winds.

Yet for Garbo it was mostly a flight from people and the present; she was full of melancholy thoughts and remorse about the path her life had taken, while for Agnetha it's exercise, a need for fresh air and time alone to ponder both practical and important things.

Neither of them found the love of their life. At least, not yet, with regard to Agnetha. Agnetha herself has never wished or aimed to be a new Garbo. She objects to the comparison – she has great respect for 'the Goddess' and her unique place in film history.

There are few people in the public eye who have been continually subjected to the tabloid press's pens for as long as Agnetha. It has happened to other celebrities for a while but usually, with a few exceptions, it comes to a quick end.

Ever since the divorce from Björn Ulvaeus, in 1978, through to her marriage to Tomas Sonnenfield in 1990 and subsequent divorce two years later, she's appeared on newspaper placards and covers. Before that, naturally, in conjunction with her own singing career and then, above all, during her time with ABBA. A total of just over twenty-five years.

Agnetha's magnetism for the press and general public is quite remarkable. Amazing stories have been made up about her. They mostly portray her as some sort of tragedienne, alone, disconsolate and forsaken, with tears in her eye-lashes.

It's possible that her song 'Om tarar vore guld' (*If Tears Were Made Of Gold*), which was such a big hit at the beginning

of the 70s, has been sitting somewhere in the global subconscious, and to some degree created the image.

The press asserts that Agnetha has contributed to her warped image by being suspicious and refusing to give interviews. She's only got herself to blame, they say. It is very seldom that any journalist has something positive to say about her wish to lead a private life in peace and not be part of the jet set. When it does occasionally happen, as it did recently when some journalists from *Expressen* and *Aftonbladet* wrote more humanely, she was very happy and noted it immediately.

She has often felt that it is futile giving interviews, as she is rarely quoted accurately. They invent slants and headlines that she didn't give them the material for. Neither is she the

kind of celebrity who needs to speak out in the press or be seen at parties and premières. On the exceptional occasions when she does it's a big deal.

It may be that it is her very shyness which makes her so attractive to people and the media. She possesses a kind of indefinable mystery. No interviews. No television interviews. No pictures. This way she has slipped into the Garbo-like aura that the weeklies describe. They often emphasise that she lives in extreme seclusion and that her home is like a secure bunker. Actually there were a lot of alarms in place when she bought it. Why should she remove them? She is constantly forced to be careful about the security of her children.

It has become a gut reaction of mine to protect myself from the press and to shield my private life to such an extent that I've completely stopped talking to the press and television. But they have still not respected my wish not to give interviews.

It's another thing altogether when it comes to my work. Then I always try to do my bit for the press. That has to be enough. I'm forced to draw the line somewhere and that's where it is. For the time being I'm not doing any work outside of the house and therefore there is no reason to give interviews. It's strange that the newspapers don't see a connection between their false revelations about my private life and my need for seclusion and security.

The attacks have not diminished through the years. Time after time I find myself spread across the newspaper placards in differing circumstances. Placards that are up for a week at a time. It makes a strong impression on people's consciousness, the wrong impression.

I see someone in the tabloids that I don't recognise, someone I don't identify as myself. They say that I am weak but I am strong and down to earth. They describe me as some sort of fool, always alone and forlorn. But I have never been forlorn! This topsy-turvy picture of me is, ultimately, an unpleasant experience. The press deceive their readers and peddle a false image of me. It's a touch ironic moreover, that you have to pay good money for it!

Sometimes I have wondered whether these muck-raking journalists, who have exploited me, among others, have ever thought about how they would react if they and their children were subjected to threats of some kind, like many of us have put up with all the time. Do they feel so secure, so autocratic, that the thought never crosses their mind that someone that they've treated really badly would like revenge? Or do they have absolutely no insight whatsoever?

Their stupid articles put the spotlight on us in a misleading way. The wrong sort of person can be drawn to us. Indirectly they expose us to danger. When, for example, the evening newspapers publish an aerial photograph of my house and its surroundings, the exact location and a plan of where all the rooms are and who sleeps in them, it's an obvious security risk.

I remember once hearing an interview with Ebba Samuelsson, then editor-in-chief of the muck-raking paper *Svensk Damtidning*. She answered one of the reporter's questions very sharply, saying that she didn't want to comment because it touched on her private life. It was respected. How privileged she is! When I answer questions in that way the immediate reaction is 'if you don't tell us we'll write it anyway'.

At home in Lidingö – 1982.

Celebrities are public people, they say, they have to accept that people are going to write about and photograph them without consent.

There are those who consider me vapid because I haven't opposed all this. But I have! A lot of reports have been sent to the Swedish Press Council and many times they have found, among others, *Svensk Damtidning* and *Hant i Veckan*, to have grossly breached good journalistic practice in articles about me. It's true that there was a short period of breathing space, but that soon ended.

In 1982 I also wrote an open letter to the press, which was later formulated into an open debate article in *Dagens Nyheter*. Among other things I wrote: 'I am a strong person, but there are limits even for me. I cherish my private life and do everything I can to protect it, not least for the sake of my children. I definitely do not belong to that group that have a habit of speaking out in the press.

I willingly go and talk to the newspapers about my work and have generally been treated objectively and quoted accurately and I value that very highly. As much as I appreciate that, I equally detest seeing myself week in, week out in interviews I did not give, with all their attendant placards and cover pictures. Is it defensible? How can it be journalistically acceptable?'

My *Dagens Nyheter* article was well-founded. Ever since the divorce from Björn Ulvaeus, four years earlier, I have been haunted by sob story reportage. It began right from the day after the divorce was announced. When I opened the blinds that morning I was met by a wall of photo flashes and couldn't go out into the garden all day. That wasn't too great.

So what is it that my children see on placard after placard? Romance here and romance there. Pregnant here and miscarriage there. Imagine my surprise, for example, when newly married to Tomas Sennenfield, instead of seeing wedding pictures I saw placards and cover pictures with 'the big news' that I was expecting a child with an actor completely unknown to me!

An American B-movie actor had spread the rumours to get publicity, having previously done something similar to Jackie Collins.

When I played Lisa, the female lead in the film *Raskenstam*, *Hänt i Veckan* published a cover picture of me which had been taken during filming. The inventive headline was 'Pregnant ABBA-Agnetha alone again'.

But 'ABBA-Agnetha' wasn't pregnant. Not alone either, actually. It was Lisa Mattson, who I played in the film, that was pregnant. The pictures were, of course, taken from the film. *Svensk Damtidning* took the opportunity to splash news of 'the romance of the year' between Gunnar Hellström and myself on its cover with the caption 'ABBA-Agnetha with her sugar daddy'. There was a picture of me from the film with a huge stomach. This is how they constantly mix fact and fiction. It's become part of the system.

I often run into people who wonder how things are after the latest newspaper headline has described how I've ended up in some pitiful situation. I'm forced to justify myself after the newspapers have made things up – even to my own children.

I have a close and open relationship with Linda and Christian. When they were small and were going to play groups and school, where their friends immediately knew if there had been anything new – often awkward

lies – in the weeklies about their mother, I had to explain things to them.

Sometimes these things were horrible, such as when the gutter press wrote that I'd had a miscarriage after the bus crash in 1983. First of all they had made up that I was pregnant because I had been buying baby clothes in a shop in London. A photographer had shadowed me and then taken pictures when I went in to the '0-12' boutique, where I'd bought clothes for the children. After the crash they thought that it was convenient to come up with the miscarriage.

Ever since some English tabloid journalists/pop veterans published the 'revealing' ABBA biography *The Name Of The Game* in 1995, which purports to tell 'the naked truth about ABBA', a number of weeklies have published a series of articles that have used the information in the scandalous book as if it were fact-based and angled them, in their special way. So the carousel started up again.

Mostly I've ignored all this stuff. I have the ability to stay above it even if I do think badly of it. What's the aim of all these speculations about my private life? Am I just an instrument for the newspapers to invent things they would like dish up for their readers in order to sell each copy?

The big question is why we who are subject to this don't get official disclaimers and replies in the same format as the newspapers. How else can the damage be repaired? I believe that the only way to put an end to the gutter press's spread is to increase the fines so much that it wouldn't pay to publish indecent reports. I felt that when I wrote in *Dagens Nyheter* and I feel the same today. It would be an intelligent way of getting rid of this kind of journalism. Currently the system is ineffective.

I have absolutely nothing against reading about people who go to premières, out on the town, and I'm pleased to look at hair cuts, clothes and check out who's keeping company with who. A lot of celebrities enjoy doing 'at-home-with' articles and I like to read them. But how can the readers differentiate between what is true and false, when in the same paper there is an innocent 'at-home-with' article and another piece based on a lie?

All it has achieved is to make me begin to read newspapers with great scepticism. An item or report might attract my interest but I end up wondering how true what they're saying really is. How objective are reports from war-torn countries and territories? Or of domestic politics, where the media wields such power to distort and influence? Why do they so seldom draw on positive stories?

Many times I've had a good laugh as I've sat at home drinking coffee by the kitchen table and read some really crazy, made-up story about myself in some paper. Today the children are big enough for us to all laugh together but, unfortunately, the laughter sometimes catches in my throat.

WHAT MAKES THE VIRTUOSO PHENOMENON SO INTERESTING TO THE PUBLIC

IS THAT THEY KNOW THE ARTIST IS WALKING ON A SLACK ROPE AND COULD FALL DOWN AND DIE *(GLEN GOULD)*

When you listen to ABBA's various recordings you can clearly hear how important Agnetha's voice is. She carries the melody on almost all of the big hits. It's like a golden thread with differing characteristics: the powerful attack at the opening, the flexible timbre, the open tones when she goes high up into treble without needing to go into falsetto.

She has a very wide register and range. Occasionally there's a kind of vulnerability in her tone, an exposed surface, which means that on some songs she hits people right in the gut. Her voice is a kind of portrait of herself.

This in itself is nothing unusual for singers. You could even say that those who don't have this quality never become truly great artists, however infallible their sense of pitch or technically competent they are.

The singing voice is the most difficult instrument of all. A guitarist can put their guitar down, a pianist can shut the lid but singers always carry their instrument with them. It influences how they feel: if the voice sounds good they feel great, if it sounds bad or is affected by a throat infection, which Agnetha catches easily, they feel wretched. Tours with a lot of live concerts in front of heaving crowds, and intensive studio work, also take their toll.

It's sink or swim for an actor's voice as well, but if their's is a little hoarse from a cold or after a late night, it just sounds 'interesting'. For a singer it's devastating, since the threat of losing their voice is always there. Yet it just can't happen on a heavily booked tour or live recordings for television. Lots of people are depending on their performance and the public's expectations of a world-famous artist are always sky high.

The voice is also a mirror of the singer's emotional state: happy, sad, angry, in love, disappointed – the emotion shows through, however skilful you are, however much command you may have.

It's ignorance about the mechanics of the voice that meant rumours could be spread saying that Agnetha and Frida hated each other so much that it caused ABBA to split. Neither of them could have sung together for ten years if they'd hated each other, it would have shown through.

To always be on form, vocally, can obviously lead to heavy mental pressure on singers. Some can't handle it and end up with performance anxiety and paralysis. Some take to drugs or start drinking. For some, a catastrophic downward spiral can begin.

Others overcome the difficulties and struggle on without lowering the demands on themselves. They are driven towards ever greater goals, forcing themselves to be better and better for their audience and themselves. When they reach out to a world-wide audience for years on end, working at the extremes of their ability, it leaves its mark on their personality, which fascinates the public.

The eccentric musical personality and pianist Glenn Gould, who became particularly well known for his superb interpretations of Bach as well as his first-rate collaborations with many jazz ensembles, cleverly formulated it thus: 'What makes the virtuoso phenomenon so interesting to the public is that they know the artist is constantly balancing high up on a slack rope without a safety net. The chances of falling down and dying are fairly high.'

Gould means that this affects every gifted artist. The chances of coming to grief are great and Agnetha has had her fair share of handling such trials.

THE DRIVING FORCE

WASN'T SO MUCH TO BE VISIBLE AS A PERSON AS TO SHOW MY TALENT

My musical home is the studio not the stage. There, in a private gathering of Björn, Benny and Frida, or just me with the musicians and sound technicians, I am in control of everything and my voice shows itself to advantage. My strength is in the studio because I can work in peace and quiet. It is there that quality comes out and ideas are born; everything is built from there. It was in the studio that ABBA best created their distinctive sound.

During the ABBA period it was Björn and Benny who wrote the music and lyrics at first, but later we started to work jointly.

The musicians had an important role to play. Each of them gave their interpretation of the tune and added twists which coloured the whole thing. Micke Tretow, naturally, meant an incredible amount to the sound. Besides his musical talent he also had a great sense of humour and is as a person always stimulating and in good spirits.

Personally I didn't write too much music during my time with ABBA, for obvious reasons. I had, of course, a home and children to take care of as well, so there wasn't any time to compose. But I put forward many artistic ideas. I've always had plenty of them inside me, and they came out during work. I came up with suggestions that gave the songs a bit of extra bite and found different ways of singing. I'm good at timing and at adding on parts. It almost happens by itself and I sense instinctively how a song should be interpreted.

We did all the choruses ourselves, with four or five overlays to get it sounding really stunning.

It's hard to tell when a hit is being made, you don't always sense it. 'Dancing Queen' was an exception, we knew immediately it was going to be massive. The same thing with 'Fernando' and 'Chiquitita' which sent shivers up the spine straight away. 'Thank You For The Music' was also very special and has a particular significance to me, because when we recorded it I was pregnant with Christian and was forced to lie down to sing it.

There are so many good songs. 'Our Last Summer' and 'When All Is Said And Done' I like a great deal, one of my other favourites is 'That's Me'. It's fantastic with its sophisticated harmonies and great chorus!

For me the best of all ABBA songs is 'The Winner Takes It All'. It has a deep personal content in the lyrics, and the music is unbeatable. Singing it was like playing a part, but I couldn't let my feelings take over. It was quite a while afterwards before I realised that we'd made a small masterpiece.

Yes, on the whole it's an impressive catalogue and I'm not surprised that ABBA are having a new lease of life. It

In the studio.

is music that will never die, it will always be around. However, I don't think that ABBA were good enough as a live band. Perhaps I'm looking too critically at our performances. They weren't choreographically well planned, we mostly worked on spontaneity and feeling.

No doubt it had its charm, being so unrehearsed stage-wise. A lot of spontaneous things happened and you can quite clearly see on the recordings whether it was a good or bad day.

In concert Frida often presented a more intense image than I, in both singing and dancing. My nervousness sometimes got in the way of my art and cut it down in a way. I didn't find it a turn on either, like a lot of people can. Nonetheless I wanted to get up on stage. It was nervy at the same time as being a kick. But the driving force wasn't so much wanting to be visible as a person as to show my talent.

This inclination to show what I was capable of was already there in my school days. I thought it was awful standing up in front of the class and reading an essay or singing. Yet even though I wanted to be swallowed up by the floor I still stayed until I had finished.

Our videos made by Lasse Hallstrom are good and the little bit of acting we did in 'ABBA – The Movie' wasn't too embarrassing. But it sometimes borders on the painful to see yourself in video recordings – I hardly ever watch them.

The ones that have been shown in Sweden are actually only a fraction of what we made. The best ones are abroad, mainly in England and the USA, and we have seldom, if ever, seen them here.

Even if it is painful to watch ABBA it's never painful to listen to us! You could pick up all the channels, lay them down on a mixing board, and listen to each and every one of them. There's nothing you can criticise. They are so extremely scrupulously made.

When I was working on my own records and composing music, both before and after ABBA, ideas came very easily to me. Often you get so into the melody that you have to look for ways of getting out of it again, see what you can add to the chorus or if it needs anything else. I can immediately hear if there are any holes that need filling. It is the little things that give a song its special tone and form: pitches, a pause, a change of phrasing, a conscious inhalation here and there.

For 'Wrap Your Arms Around Me' I'd written a song called 'Man'. It took a long time before I could approve it. The same thing for 'I Won't Let You Go' on 'Eyes Of A Woman'. A lot of people think that you write a song in an afternoon but, in general, just getting started on the composing is hard work. I need to be completely by myself because it's hard, intense work, so I have to deliberatley set aside time for it.

The lyrics are very important to me. When I see a sentence in front of me I 'hear' the music within me and write it down. I'm always getting lots f ideas and trying out different little things. However, I never compare what I compose with things someone else has done. First and foremost it's me that decides if it's good or bad.

People often ask me who, out of all composers, pop and rock stars, I like most. There is, of course, a whole list of people I'd gladly name. When it comes to composers and lyricists I put Lennon/McCartner foremost. But nonetheless Björn and Benny are closest to my heart. If there was a Nobel prize for pop music and musicals they ought to get it!

I THINK A LOT ABOUT LIFE

AND WHAT IT ALL MEANS

When I want to relax I generally do so with a book. Just as soon as I've closed the cover of one I start another. I'm not well acquainted with pure literature and don't really have any cultural reference points other than those I've created myself within the world of pop.

I think a lot about life and what it all means. I'm searching for something to pursue. There are three topics that I love to engross myself in and read advanced books about. They are yoga, astrology and Ayur-Vedic medicine.

Yoga is a way of life and gives life purpose. I wish that I'd discovered it a long time ago. Not least for breathing exercises. Imagine, I could have made good use of it in ABBA, which involved so many time changes, so much stress and nervousness, so much concentration and winding down.

I think of the awful hours before a live concert when your nerves are all jittery and you tried to settle them with champagne. Loneliness weighs heavily just before a big performance. It would have been fantastic to have been familiar with yoga then, because my nerves can take the edge off of my ability to perform live. It became the norm to go on stage anyway and naturally they disappeared after a while.

I didn't experience anything like that pressure when I made videos and films or was in the studio. It was always live performances that made me shaky and the yogic breathing exercises would have helped me greatly. Most of the time, by the way, we breathe incorrectly. Doing yoga you learn three different breathing techniques, which are fantastically good for you. You also exercise your heart, stretch muscles which you otherwise don't use, meditate and relax. It's even said that meditation lowers cholesterol levels.

Through the breathing you get inside yourself, and can redress the balance when you've lost your equilibrium. It's not possible to be in control of every situation in your life, but yoga gives you something to fall back on. That's how I get my strength and find a balance between body and soul. Also, one advantage is that you can practice it anywhere. It doesn't require any special instruments or equipment, so if I'd known yoga when ABBA was in full swing it would have been easy to practise in the hotels or during journeys.

Now I have learnt that if, for example, I get a headache then I don't immediately take a headache tablet but try to find out what the root of the complaint is, instead of immediately attempting to cure the symptoms with some pills. It's the same for anxiety, which can be felt as a physical pain. It's a warning sign that something has gone wrong in your life. Even here you have to find the core of the problem, rather than cramming yourself with sedatives.

Obviously there are occasions when the doctor has to prescribe medicines but it only solves the problem on a superficial level. You still have to come to grips with the deeper causes. This is where yoga is effective in helping me reach them.

Ayur-Vedic medicine also plays a big role in my life. I'm not saying that it guarantees good health, but it can be used in preventing the need for medical treatment. Among others I have read a book by the Indian Deepak Chopra, called *Perfect Health*, which I often refer to.

Chopra is an Ayur -Vedic doctor who has also qualified as a doctor in the West. He has a balanced insight. For example, he criticises Western medical science for not looking at the person as a whole. That is, it lacks a holistic view. What he writes fascinates me. For a considerable improvement in health Chopra says that we need a new kind of knowledge based on a more profound view of life. His books provide a source of such knowledge, a system of preventative medicine and health care, which is called Maharishi Ayur-Veda.

It comes from India and goes back five thousand years. I wish that there was more of this way of thinking in medical treatment today.

There are a few lines in Chopra's book, *Perfect Health*, that I often re-read. He talks about how we shouldn't see ourselves as isolated organisms in time and space, rather as cells in the cosmic body. This is what he says, among other things:

'On the level of quantum mechanics there is a sharp line dividing you from the rest of the Universe. Every one of us balances between the infinitely large and the infinitely small. The same protons that are found within stars have existed for at least five billion years and are also within us. The neutrinos which flash through the Earth in a few millionths of a second are, for a short period, part of us. You are a river of atoms and molecules that have come from all corners of the Cosmos. You are an excrescence of energy, whose waves stretch out into the whole field's outer edges. You are a reservoir of intelligence that cannot be emptied, because Nature as a whole cannot be emptied.'

Ideas like this are so captivating. I get a lot out of them; they broaden my consciousness. I have also got into astrology, and like to read books on the subject. It is certainly the oldest of the sciences with roots in ancient China and ancient India.

Knowledge of the planets' and stars' influence on the Earth and its people was an integral part of everyday life. The knowledge that can be gained from astrology makes it easier to understand yourself and other people. The importance of this cannot be overstated.

Astrology is 'trendy' these days. Perhaps people are looking at it again because of a lack of anything else to believe in. There is little trace of Christianity in our country. My interest in astrology is not such that I use it in place of religion, or everyday thinking. Nor is my first question, when I meet someone new, what sign was he or she born under. Although it can be tempting...

I think that there is a lot in astrology that makes sense. When I read about Aries, which is my sign, I can't help but give a smile of recognition. In Ulla Sallert's book *ASTROLOGY – A Way Of Life* it states, among other things, about Ariens, that they are full of energy and will power, are restless and have little patience. They like to come first, are serious and energetic about optional projects but become stifled by routine work. They have sudden mood swings and can flare up and in their need for honesty can say things that are hurtful.

Ulla Sallert also writes that the need for independence in Ariens is strong, they like to go their own way. In love they find it difficult to commit to anyone and have a strong need for integrity in relationships.

A lot of this fits in with what I'm like. I really do have an enormous need for freedom, freedom on all levels. I want my innermost space to be left in peace. In relation to men I sometimes can't help feeling a superiority, which has to do with maturity and experience, both as a parent and economically. It is perhaps due to the fact that I have been through so much. More joy, sorrow, success, money, disappointments.

I believe that a lot of working women have this problem. It's not surprising that there is often a schism between men and women. We are so different and we often talk at cross purposes. It's important to be able to talk to each other. Men go through crises, too. They are often afraid to open up in case they lose control. It can become a tacit power struggle, with barriers that are hard to tear down.

I could never become fanatical about these interests I have mentioned, but what I'm looking for is knowledge and insight. I am quite simply trying to pick out the things I think suit me and enrich my life.

THERE WAS A TIME

WHEN THE MUSIC FELL SILENT. BOTH WITHIN ME AND AROUND ME

There was a time when the music fell silent. Both within me and around me. During a ten year period I neither played, sang nor listened to music. I didn't even bother to get a decent stereo system. I was tired of composing and tired of singing. I didn't feel that there were any challenges in music for me. Although I did occasionally listen when good new stuff came along, it was as if I'd had too much of everything. During this time, after ABBA and my own LPs, other things started to come into my life. Yoga for example. I needed peace and quiet instead of noise.

Now, again, I feel that I can begin to enjoy both ABBA and some of my own things as well as other artists. I suddenly feel a desire to listen again.

You can't re-awaken the yearning for music straight away, it has to mature and develop. Really, it would have been easy to let myself get pushed into it, because now and then I get offers of work. But nothing good enough, nothing novel that felt exciting.

At the same time as interest in ABBA was rekindled around the world, I, too, began to get something out of the music again. At some point Frida said the same thing. We had worked so much with ABBA that we had no urge to listen to the music.

Now Sony Music and Micke Tretow have issued a CD box set of songs that I'd done on my own down the years and it feels nice to hear them again. After all I'd written most of the material myself. 'Elva kvinnor i ett hus' and the LPs I did with Linda and Christian, 'Nu tandas tusen juleljus' (*A tTousand Christmas Candles Are Being Lit*) and 'Kom folj med i var karusell' (*Come Along On Our Roundabout*), were produced by me, too.

Sometimes I get the urge to do something again. A few years ago it was totally inconceivable. Never again, I thought then. However, quiet times can also be creative. For example, working on this book I can feel myself hankering after something more. It's good for the brain to work, good to ponder on the past and the future; to express yourself.

I am conscious of having a special voice and I am confident in the studio. So, there are days when it feels tempting to try something again. Now that I have a certain distance from my music I listen to it differently. I can feel, analyse and respond in a fresh way.

Musically, my dream would be to sing the theme song to an outstanding television series or film. I still have a great interest in cinematics. I would like to see something different, perhaps work on something myself. A romance, maybe, where the main ingredient isn't just sex but ardent sensuality. I think they've lost the serenity, the breathtaking tension that can exist between a man and a woman without them even touching each other.

It feels good to think of the people who have believed in me through the years. Little Gerhard, who discovered me and helped me get on. Everyone at Cupol. Sven-Olof Walldorf. That was such a great time. Gunnar Hellstrom also believed in me with regard to acting and film. However, there have not been too many people along the way who have had the vision or capacity to express it, who have seen me in the right way, who have had a vision of what could be and grabbed it.

The last few years have been a time of thinking and searching for me, which is probably nothing unique among people in their forties. However, in my life such an immense number of experiences and adventures have been squeezed into a relatively short space of time. More has gone on than is normally granted in a whole lifetime.

Yes, the silence has been necessary. It's interesting, because it has perhaps been a way for me to digest everything, a kind of recovery. This is where the walks have been so important. It cleanses the mind and helps you think.

A lot of people wonder if ABBA will ever make a come-back, whether we can imagine doing anything together. I feel that each thing has its day. ABBA needs a rest. What will be, will be. Perhaps we need to let go of the urge to do something in order to allow it to mature in peace.

When myths begin to grow up around you – such as the Garbo stamp the press have put on me – it can involve a certain danger. People can get the idea that you have closed all the doors behind you and are no longer interested in anything. But I haven't closed any doors, not to myself, ideas, film opportunities or my songs.

I just feel that I don't want to be seen in any particular way. It would be horrible to be compelled to live up to a world-wide reputation, to the money or to what other people expect of you.

Sometimes I hear: start flying, start singing, start I don't know what! I'm not afraid of changes. For better or worse they are a part of life.

But I must be allowed to be as I am.

Agnetha Fältskog

Som jag är

AGNETHA FÄLTSKOG

DISCOGRAPHY
BY BJÖRN WALDENSTRÖM

Apart from ABBA Agnetha has made a lot of records and had a lot of success as a solo artist. On the record label Cupol she released singles and LPs, several of which got into the Swedish charts. Most of them were her own compositions. The changeover to Polar, which, of course, was only natural after ABBA formed, was not fully completed until after the last Cupol release in 1979. She had been recording with ABBA members on the Polar label, with CBS-Cupol's permission, since 1970.

The launch on to the German market at the end of the sixties resulted in a number of singles. A few were German versions of songs from her Swedish repertoire but most of them were purely German productions.

After the years with ABBA Agnetha continued as a solo artist on Polar, changing to WEA in 1987.

Her records were released in a number of countries, not only Europe. Records by Agnetha were available in, for example, Japan, Australia, New Zealand, South Africa, Mexico and the USA. She recorded a few songs in Spanish, for among others the South American market, something ABBA did in their time with some success.

The discography of Agnetha's records includes all her Swedish and German records and lists which records came out with songs in Spanish. The notation (-) indicates that the record was not released with a picture cover.

	Company	Issue No.	Year
SWEDEN SINGLES			
Följ med mig/Jag var så kär	Cupol	CS 211	1967
Slutet gott, allting gott/Utan dej	Cupol	CS 217	1968
En sommar med dej/Försonade	Cupol	CS 233	1968
Allting har förändrat sig/			
Den jag väntat på	Cupol	CS 236	1968
Sjung denna sång/			
Någonting händer med mej			
(Duets with Jörgen Edman)	Cupol	CS 239	1968
Snövit och de sju dvärgarna/			
Min farbror Jonathan	Cupol	CS 244	1968
En gång fanns bara vi två/			
Fram för svenska sommaren	Cupol	CS 250	1969
	Cupol	CS 256	1969
Zigenarvän/Som en vind kom			
du till mej	Cupol	CS 260	1969
Om tårar vore guld/Litet solskensbarn	Cupol	CS 264	1970
Ta det bara med ro/Som ett eko	Cupol	CS 272	1970
Kungens vaktparad/Jag vill att			
du skall bli lycklig	Cupol	CS 277	1971
Många gånger än/Han lämnar			
mig för att komma till dig	Cupol	CS 278	1971
Vart skall min kärlek föra/			
Nu skall du bli stilla	Cupol	CS 284	1972
Tio mil kvar till Korpilombolo/			
Sä glad som dina ogon	Cupol	CS 291	1972
En sang om sorg och glädje/Vi			
har hunnit fram till refrangen	Cupol	CS 297	1973
Golliwog/Came for your love			
(= Here for your love)	Cupol	CS 299	1974
Gulleplutt/Dom har glomt	Cupol	CS 301	1974
S.O.S./Visa i åttonde månaden	Cupol	CUS 303	1975

	Company	Issue No.	Year
När du tar mej i din famn/			
Jag var så kär (from 1968) (-)	Cupol	CUS 304	1979

Note. Many of the Cupol records were also released in Norway. CBS-Cupol also released, specially for the Norwegian market, a few singles with different songs, taken from Swedish LPs. As far as it is known they did not have picture covers.

CAMPAIGN RECORD

	Company	Issue No.	Year
Borsta tandtrollen bort (single-sided single designed to be distributed to children in connection with a dental hygiene campaign.) Produced by Cupol but not bearing the Cupol emblem on the label (-)	Cupol	CSR 2	1968

SINGLES

	Company	Issue No.	Year
Never again (Duet with Tomas Ledin/			
(Tomas Ledin: Just For Fun)	Polar	POS 1308	1982
The Heat Is On/Man	Polar	POS 1335	1983
Can't Shake Loose/To Love	Polar	POS 1345	1983
It's So Nice To Be Rich/P & B			
(From the SF film 'P & B')	Polar	POS 1347	1983
I Won't Let You Go/You're There	Polar	POS 1366	1985
One Way Love/			
Turn the World Around	Polar	POS 1373	1985
The Way You Are/Fly Like the Eagle			
(Duets with Ola Håkansson)	Sonet	SON 2317	1986
På söndag/Mitt namn är Blom			
(With her son Christian)	WEA	248 271-7	1987
Karusellvisan/Liten och trött			
(With her son Christian) (-)	WEA	248 100-7	1987

	Company	Issue No.	Year
The Last Time/Are You Gonna			
Throw It All Away	WEA	248 136-7	1987
I Wasn't The One			
(Duet with Peter Cetera)/			
If You Need Somebody Tonight	WEA	248 046-7	1988
Let It Shine (remixed version)/			
Maybe It Was Magic	WEA	247 720-7	1988

12" SINGLES

	Company	Issue No.	Year
The Heat Is On (extended version)/Man	Polar	POLM 5	1983
The Way You Are (extended version)/			
The Way You Are (instrumental)/			
The Way You Are			
(with Ola Hakansson)	Sonet	12T10223	1986
The Last Time (remix)/The Last Time/			
Are You Gonna Throw It All Away	WEA	248 087-0	1988
I Wasn't The One (extended remix)/			
Yo no fui/			
If You Need Somebody Tonight	WEA	247 931-0	1988
Let It Shine (extended remix)/			
Let It Shine/Maybe It Was Magic	WEA	247 719-0	1988

LPs

	Company	Issue No.	Year
Agnetha Fältskog	Cupol	CLP 64	1968
Agnetha Fältskog Vol. 2	Cupol	CLP 80	1969
Som jag är	Cupol	CLP 345	1970
När en vacker tanke blir en sang	Cupol	CLPN 348	1971
Agnetha Fältskogs bästa (compilation)	Cupol	CLPN 1023	1973
Elva kvinnor i ett hus	Cupol	CLPS 351	1975
Tio är med Agnetha			
(compilation + 1 new recording)	Cupol	CLPS 352	1979

	Company	Issue No.	Year
Sjung denna säng (compilation)	Cupol	CLPM 5041	1986

Note. The first three LPs were reissued in the early 1970s. New serial no.s CLPL 1002,1003,1016)

	Company	Issue No.	Year
Nu tändas tusen juleljus			
(with her daughter Linda,			
recorded 1980)	Polar	POLS 328	1981
Wrap Your Arms Around Me	Polar	POLS 365	1983
Eyes of a Woman	Polar	POLS 385	1985
Kom följ med i var karusell			
(with her son Christian)	Polar	242 186-1	1987
I Stand Alone	WEA	242 231-1	1987

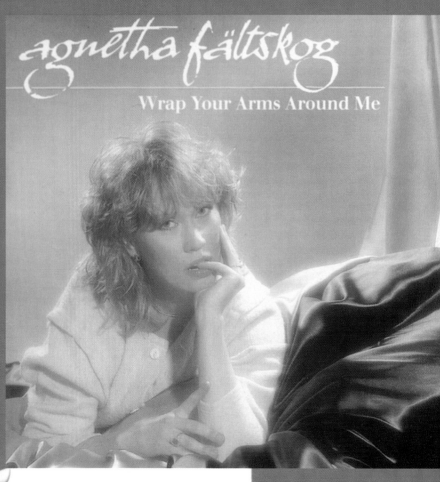

	Company	Issue No.	Year

FORIEGN LP RELEASES
SOLD IN SWEDISH SHOPS

	Company	Issue No.	Year
Agnetha (From Holland, same			
content as Cupol CLPN 348)	Embassy	EMB 31094	1974
Agnetha collection			
(From Finland, compilation			
of Swedish songs)	Kaktus	KAKLP 10	1986

OTHER SWEDISH LPs TO WHICH AGNETHA CONTRIBUTES

	Company	Issue No.	Year
Jorgen Edman			
(contains songs from the			
Cupol single CLPN 239)	Cupol	CLP 79	1969
Jesus Christ Superstar			
(dbl. LP with contributions			
by Agnetha)	Philips	6675 002	1972
Ulf Lundell Nådens år			
(1 recording with Agnetha			
involved)	Parlaphone	35550	1978
Ulf Lundell Dådens år			
(1 recording with Agnetha			
involved)	Parlaphone	35620	1978
Tomas Ledin The human touch			
(1 recording with Agnetha)	Polar	POLS 364	1982

Note. Some compilations with various artists also exist with Agnetha on them. This discography is only concerned with releases from her normal recordings.

CASSETTES – LPs

Later LPs were also released as cassettes, with the same serial number as their respective LPs.

CASSETTES – SPECIALLY
SELECTED COMPILATIONS

	Company	Issue No.	Year
Det bästa från Svensktoppen 1			
(2 recordings by Agnetha, and			
photo cover)	Frituna	FRLK 007	1980
Agnetha Fältskog 1			
(in the Team Toppen series)	Marian	MK 2135	1985
Agnetha Fältskog med gäster, Vol. 1			
(8 recordings by Agnetha)	TMC	TMCG 889	1988

CDs
LPs RELEASED AS CDs

	Company	Issue No.	Year
Tio år med Agnetha (from 1979)	CBS	465298-2	1980
Nu tändas tusen juleljus (from 1980)	Polar	POLCD 328	1987
Wrap Your Arms Around Me (from 1983)	Polar	POLCD 365	1988
Eyes of a Woman (from 1985)	Polar	POLCD 385	1988
Kom följ med i vår karusell			
(Simultaneous LP CD)	WEA	242 186-2	1987
I Stand Alone (Simultaneous LP CD)	WEA	242 231-2	1987

CD COMPILATIONS

	Company	Issue No.	Year
Julens musik (incl. the LP			
Nu tändas tusen juleljus from 1980)	Polar	521 347-2	1994
Polars roliga timme (Agnetha: Ljuva			
sextital, radio recording from 1980)	Polar	521 797-2	1994
Agnetha Björn Benny Annifrid			
på svenska	Polar	521 809-2	1994

GERMAN SINGLES

	Company	Issue No.	Year
Robinson Crusoe/Sonny Boy	Metronome	M 25056	1968
Señor Gonzales/			
Mein schönster Tag	Metronome	M 25108	1968
Concerto d'Amore/Wie der Wind	Metronome	M 25125	1969
Das Fest der Pompadour/			
Wer schreibt heut' noch			
Liebesbriefe	Metronom	M 25138	1969
Fragezeichen mag ich nicht/			
Wie der nächste Autobus	Metronome	M 25186	1970
Ein kleiner Mann in einer Flasche/			
Ich suchte Liebe bei dir	Metronome	M 25243	1970
Geh' mit Gott/Tausend Wunder	CBS	S 7494	1972
Komm doch zu mir/Ich denk' an dich	CBS	S 8415	1972
Golliwog/Here For Your Love			
(English Iyrics)	Epic	EPC 2444	1974

GERMAN CDs

	Company	Issue No.	Year
Geh mit Gott (compilation of			
16 German language songs)	Royal Records	1994 001	1994

OTHER COUNTRIES ABROAD

To annotate all the foreign releases of Agnetha's recordings would not only take up too much space, the list could never be made complete. Here only Agnetha's Spanish recordings will be listed, which along with English and German is the only foreign language she has sung in. The records were made for Spain and Argentina.

RECORDINGS IN SPANISH

	Company	Issue No.	Year
Single: Ya nunca más			
(Duet with Tomas Ledin)/			
+ 1 (Tomas L.)	Victoria, Spain	22S 0549	1983
Single: Ya nunca más			
(Duet with Tomas Ledin)/			
+ 1 (Tomas L.)	RCA, Argentina	E 0259	1983
Single: Yo no fui/			
I Wasn't the One			
(promotional) (-)	WEA, Spain	WEA 983	1987
Single: Yo no fui/			
(+ another artist)			
(promotion) (-)	WEA, Argentina	DFW 112	1987
Single: La ultima vez/			
(+ another artist)			
(promotion) (-)	WEA, Argentina	DFW 121	1987
LP: Estoy sola			
(= LP I Stand Alone,			
with Yo no fui)	WEA, Argentina	80710	1987

And finally, there are two picture discs worth noting for their collectability:

PICTURE DISCS FROM ENGLAND

	Company	Issue No.	Year
The Heat is on/Man	Epic	WA 3436	1983
Can't Shake Loose/To love	Epic	WA 3812	1983

ABBA - DISCOGRAPHY

The Singles

People Need Love/Merry-Go-Round 1972

He Is Your Brother/Santa Rosa 1972

Love Isn't Easy/I Am Just A Girl 1973

Ring Ring (Bara Du Slog En Signal)/Ah Vilka Tider 1973

Ring Ring (English)/Merry-Go-Round 1973

So Long/I've Been Waiting For You 1974

I Do, I Do, I Do, I Do, I Do/Rock Me 1975

S.O.S./Man In The Middle 1975

Waterloo/Honey Honey (both sung in Swedish) 1974

Waterloo (English)/Watch Out...1974

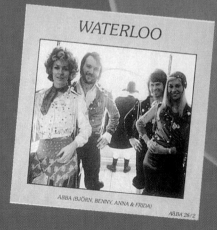

Mamma Mia/Intermezzo No. 1 1975

Honey, Honey/King Kong Song 1974

Fernando/Hey, Hey, Helen 1976

Dancing Queen/That's Me...................1976

Money, Money, Money/Crazy World...1976

Knowing Me, Knowing You/

Happy Hawaii.....................................1977

The Name Of The Game/

Wonder (Departure)............................1977

Take A Chance On Me/

I'm A Marionette 1977

Eagle/Thank You For The Music..........1977

Summernight City/Medley...................1978

Chiquitita/Lovelight.............................1979

Voulez-Vous/Does Your Mother

Know (twelve-inch) 1979

Does Your Mother Know/

Kisses Of Fire 1979

Voulez-Vous/Angeleyes 1979

Gimme!Gimme!Gimme!

(A Man After Midnight)/

The King Has Lost His Crown 1979

I Have A Dream/Take A Chance On Me

(live) 1979

The Winner Takes It All/Elaine 1980

Super Trouper/The Piper 1980

Lay All Your Love On Me/

On And On And On (twelve-inch)....1981

One Of Us/Should I Laugh Or Cry......1981

Head Over Heels/The Visitors 1982

The Day Before You Came/

Cassandra 1982

Under Attack/You Owe Me One 1982

Dancing Queen/

Lay All Your Love On Me 1992

Voulez-Vous/Summernight City 1992

Thank You For The Music/

Happy New Year................................1992

The Albums

Ring Ring	UK: Polydor 843 642-2	1973
Waterloo	UK: Polydor 843 643-2	1974
ABBA	UK: Polydor 831 596-2	1975
Greatest Hits	UK: Epic CDEPC 10017	1975
Arrival	UK: Polydor 821 319-2	1976
ABBA: The Album	UK: Polydor 821 217-2	1977
Voulez-Vous	UK: Polydor 821 320-2	1979
Greatest Hits Vol. 2	UK: Polydor 800 012-2	1979
Gracias Por La Musica	Japan:Polydor POCP 2209	1980
Super Trouper	UK: Polydor 800 023-2	1980
The Visitors	UK: Polydor 800 011-2	1981
The Singles - The First Ten Years	UK: Polydor 810 050-2	1982
ABBA Live	UK:Polydor 829 951-2	1986
ABBA Gold	UK:Polydor 517 007-2	1992
More ABBA Gold	UK: Polydor 519 353-2	1993

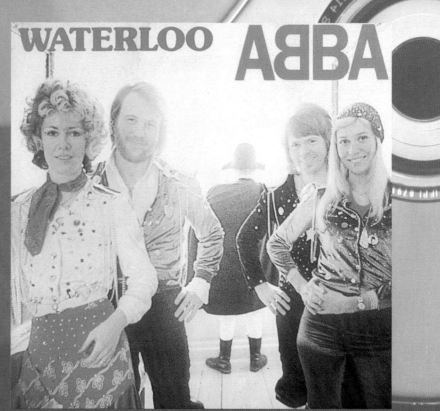

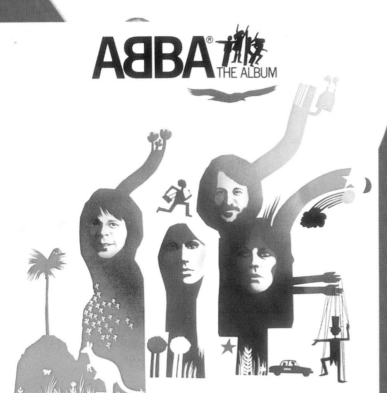

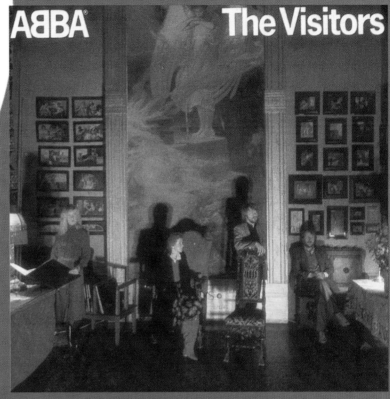